The Guide

The aim of this guide to the *Camino Mozárabe* or '
of churches, monasteries, historic monuments, t
interest along the way and suggestions as to where to eat aɪɪu ᴏ.ᴏᴏ,
sketch maps, plus an overview of the route, though more detailed ones are available ɪɪɪ
the guide books listed on page 9. The present volume is designed to accompany (not
replace) existing route-finding guides and is not intended specifically for any one type of
user, either, whether walker, cyclist, rider, motorist or those using public transport;
however, because it has been prepared by a walker it will inevitably reflect this mode of
transport. Much of the *Vía de la Plata* is accessible to those on mountain bikes, though
riders will need to dismount on certain stretches and be prepared to lift their machines
over gates on others. Details of cycle repair shops (CRS) are given where known.

History and Background

Although the *Camino Francés* or so-called "French road" is the most well-known, well-
travelled and well-documented of the pilgrim roads to Santiago de Compostela (and to
such an extent that for many people it is the only one), it was, in fact, only one of several
used in former times. Pilgrims in the past obviously did not travel to Roncesvalles by train
or bus to begin their journey there, as do their modern counterparts, but set out on foot
from their own front doors and as well as the northern coastal route, for example, the
Camino Aragonés over the Somport pass to Puenta la Reina, routes from the east of
Spain and several roads through Portugal, there was also the *Camino Mozárabe* or *Vía de
la Plata*. This was so named, it is now thought, *not* because it followed the old Roman
silver route from Huelva in the south to Astorga in the north but as a corruption of the
Arabic *bal'latta*, a term used to describe wide, paved or public roads. This route, with its
own network of tributaries, took pilgrims from Seville and other places, both along the way
and adjacent to it, through Mérida, Cáceres and Salamanca to Zamora. (Modern pilgrims
who wish to begin their journey in Granada, for example, now have a waymarked route at
their disposal and a CSJ route-finding guide to describe it.) From there many continued
north via Benavente and La Bañeza to Astorga to join the main flux of European pilgrims
coming from the Pyrenees. Others deviated via Puebla de Sanabria and Ourense to go
directly to Santiago through Galicia. It is sometimes suggested that this was to avoid
the Montes de León and the stiff climb up to O Cebreiro but as the route through the
western part of the province of Zamora and the province of Ourense is extremely
strenuous and necessitates climbing up (and down again) both the Puerto de Padornelo
(1368m) and then the pass at A Canda (1268m) on two successive days, this is not a very
plausible explanation. There was also the further option of going through northern
Portugal, via Bragança, to rejoin the route through Galicia in Verín. (This variant - the
Camino Portugués de la Vía de la Plata - has also been fully waymarked and a CSJ guide
is in preparation.)

The original *Vía de la Plata* was a Roman road, running in more or less a straight line
south–north from Mérida to Gijón, and anyone walking this route to Santiago today will be
very much aware of being in Roman Spain. It was in two distinct parts: a paved section as
far as Salamanca and a compressed earth track from there to Astorga and onwards. A
section of the original paved road has been restored, about a kilometre leading uphill out
of the small spa town of Baños de Montemayor on the boundary between Extremadura

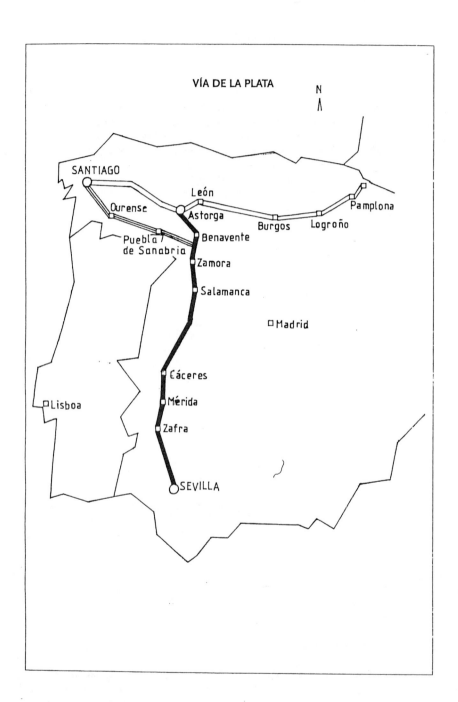

VÍA DE LA PLATA

and Castilla-León, and gives us an idea of the surface on the first part of the route. The Romans also built innumerable bridges along the way, many of which are still standing. Some of these are quite simple ones, like those at Casas de Don Antonio and Valdesalor (both south of Cáceres), the one over the Río Turienzo near Estación de Valderrey (shortly before you reach Astorga) or the much longer and more elaborate constructions such as the bridges over the Río Tormes in Salamanca, the Duero in Zamora and the Guadiana in Mérida, the latter being 792m long, with its 60 arches. (This is the way pilgrims enter the town. Mérida did not have just one Roman bridge, though, as pilgrims left the town by another one too – over the Río Alberragas to the north.)

The entire Roman route was also divided into stages of 20–25 Roman miles, with a *mansio* or place where travellers could rest overnight at the end of each one. The route was marked with *miliarios*, milestones, one every "1000 steps" or 1472m, and a number of them are still visible with their markings on them; these stood some 76cm (2ft 6in) high, like stone pillars, and were engraved with a Roman numeral. Several of them are still standing too, especially in the area near the Puente de la Magdalena, below Calzada de Béjar. Numbers CXLVIII (148) and CXLIX (149) were repositioned in 1994 by the local "Amigos" of Fuenterroble de Salvatierra (some 50km south of Salamanca), and relevant *ayuntamientos* (town halls) have plans to reinstate others along the route as well.

The Romans did not invent this route completely from scratch, however, any more than the pilgrims, whether on the *Camino francés* or the *Vía de la Plata*, created a completely new road to take them to Santiago, but they both used and improved on existing paths and tracks instead. (A lot of research done on the *Vía de la Plata* has been carried out by people interested in Roman roads, rather than pilgrim routes.) The Romans who came to the south of Spain arrived by boat, from southern Italy, and could sail up the Guadalquivir river as at that time it was navigable not only as far as Seville but beyond as well. The road that became the *Vía de la Plata* originally started in Mérida, the town known as Augusta Emerita, which they developed for their emeritus or pensioned-off soldiers from the fifth and tenth legions, and this road was used as a means of moving troops northwards. Later on it was extended as far south as Seville. There are an enormous number of Roman remains all along the *Vía de la Plata*, starting with the city of Italica on the outskirts of Seville, and especially in Mérida, with its theatre (still used for performances today) which originally held 3,000 spectators, an amphitheatre with seating for 14,000 and a circus which could accommodate 30,000 people. Mérida also has a splendid Roman museum and the so-called Acueducto de los Milagros (a look at it will reveal why) and its two Roman reservoirs, one of which, the Embalse de Proserpina, nowadays used as a recreation area, is a few kilometres to the north of the city on the route of the *Vía de la Plata* itself. Anyone who is interested in things Roman could follow the *Vía de la Plata* (in a car, for example) just for this reason. The Roman features are not limited to the Seville–Astorga section either – the *termas* (hot springs) in Ourense, for example, were also in use in Roman times and there are several bridges of Roman origin in other places along that route too.

So much for the Roman aspects. The route they established forms the physical basis of the one that interests us, the route which pilgrims in future centuries would take. Pilgrims from the south of Spain and other parts of the Christian Mediterranean world (who travelled to Seville by boat), as well as Arabs and Orientals, apparently, made use of the existing Roman road infrastructure to take them to Santiago. This *camino* (the *Vía de la Plata*) – a great Roman engineering feat – also had its own network of tributaries, as already indicated: from Córdoba, for example, and Granada, joining the route in Mérida, or from Toledo, where pilgrims joined it in Salamanca. It is often thought that pilgrims to Santiago only used the *Vía de la Plata after* the *Reconquista* (in 1492) but they actually began much earlier. The *Vía de la Plata* as a pilgrim artery began in the twelfth century, after the fall of Toledo in 1085, but especially after the political and religious annexation by Galicia of a large part of the western fringe of Spain through which the *Vía de la Plata* ran – the area around Salamanca, for example. Another important influence in "getting the pilgrimage off the ground" along this route was the powerful Archbishop of Santiago, Gelmírez. It is already well known how he was responsible for promoting the *Camino Francés* across the north of Spain but under his rule the diocese of Santiago de Compostela, which already reached to Salamanca, was extended as far south as Mérida in 1179. Spain was still largely under Muslim rule, of course, but during this period there was a degree of tolerance allowed to Christians – the Mozarabic ones, those living under Muslim rule (as opposed to the Mudéjar Muslims living later under Christian domination) – and the *Vía de la Plata* was the route these pilgrims took to Santiago, hence the name *Camino Mozárabe.* The *Vía de la Plata* was also the route used in 1062 (under Fernando I) to take the body of Saint Isidore of Seville up to León and after the reconquest of Córdoba, the bells of Santiago cathedral, which had been taken to the mosque in Córdoba 200 years previously by Al-Mansur, were returned via this route to their rightful home in Galicia.

The movement of pilgrims along the *Vía de la Plata* was never as great as along the *Camino Francés* but it too had its own infrastructure of pilgrim hospitals. The question is often raised as to the existence of Jacobean churches or other pilgrim influences along this route. Once again, there are not as many as there are on the *Camino Francés* (one explanation that has been suggested is that the Mozarabic pilgrims were exiles/refugees and thus had no time to leave permanent traces of their passage) but there are certainly a significant number and the interested reader is referred to the summary in the central insert. The other important factor to remember, when considering the historical aspects of the pilgrimage along the *Vía de la Plata*, is the role played by the Order of the Knights of Santiago, founded in Cáceres in 1170 and one of whose purposes was to protect pilgrims on their way.

The Vía de la Plata today

The route from Seville to Astorga has been waymarked (very thoroughly and clearly) since 1991, when the late Andrés Muñoz Garde researched the route and painted yellow arrows, like those on the *Camino Francés*, to guide a large group he was leading along this stretch of the *Vía de la Plata*. He was the one person who really set the route on its feet again in recent times. People living along the way are sometimes heard to remark "Ah, yes, now there is a new route to Santiago," assuming it must be something that has been invented recently but, although it has been waymarked for nearly 15 years now, very few pilgrims used it in the early years. The other catalyst was the very active group of Amigos del Camino de Santiago in Seville, led by the late José Luis Salvador Salvador, who not only continued and maintained the waymarking but also visited all the villages along the way within reasonable walking distance of each other, talking to priests, *alcaldes* (mayors), the local police and so on to set up a network of very basic sleeping accommodation in parish halls, schools, sports centres etc., so that nowadays, apart from large towns, there is always somewhere (often very spartan, obviously) for pilgrims to sleep, in addition to *hostales*, and *fondas* where these exist. The Seville "Amigos" also produce a special *credencial*, a "pilgrim passport" for the route (see below). There are also several other associations of "Amigos de la Vía de la Plata" along the way (those in Fuenterroble de Salvatierra and Zamora are particularly active) whilst the group in Ourense played a big part in clearing and signposting the now very well-waymarked route through Galicia.

In 1992 only about 50 people walked the route in a whole year (the editor of this guide was one of them) and it was quite different then, not only from the well-travelled *Camino Francés* but also from the route today. Nowadays people living along the route know who pilgrims are, where they are going, what the yellow arrows are for and that they are living along an important pilgrim road to Santiago. There are also many more pilgrims – relatively speaking, of course. In 1993, a Holy Year there were about 100 (compared with 99,000 on the *Camino Francés*), some 450 in 1996 and what was often described by local people as *un montón* (a "huge number") in the 1999 Holy Year – about 3000 altogether. This compares with over 155,000 on the *Camino Francés* in 1999 and 65,000 in the year 2002, in which year there were some 4,000 pilgrims recorded by the cathedral authorities in Santiago as having arrived via the *Vía de la Plata*. and more than 5,000 in 2003. Many of these did not walk (or cycle) all the way from Seville but, like those who start in Sarria on foot on the *Camino Francés* in order to walk the minimum 100km required to qualify for their *compostela*, many of them started in Ourense for the same reason, and in 2004 5616 of the total of 9,309 pilgrims who arrived in Santiago along the *Camino Mozárabe* did exactly this. A lot of people also start either in or after A Gudiña because the Xunta de Galicia (regional government) has set up a certain number of *refugios*, which obviously makes it much easier to walk the route. There are few *first time* pilgrims on the *Vía de la Plata* at present, though, and it is still surprisingly uncommon for people who live along the route itself to set out from their own front doors and make their first journey to Santiago along a *camino* which would lead them there directly. For some reason, perhaps because of the massive publicity during the nineties about the *Camino Francés* being **the** *Camino de Santiago* rather than just one of many routes to the "city of the apostle", people seem to think that they should go to Roncesvalles (from Seville, for example!) to set out on the "proper *Camino*, though this is gradually changing. Others are misinformed, thinking that the route from Seville is not waymarked, or that the *Vía de la Plata* is all road walking, since the N630, the main road which in fact follows the historical route taken by the *Vía de la Plata*, is confusingly also named *"Ruta de la Plata"*. Other people are unwilling to follow a route where "there are no *refugios*." In the past there were also no guidebooks, nobody, even priests and people with yellow arrows outside their doors, knew about the route or where it went, and anybody walking along with a rucksack bigger than a daysack was automatically either a "hippie", a tramp or a *transeunte* (somebody walking from town to town theoretically in search of work) and looked at often very oddly by people in shops and places with accommodation. And unlike the *Camino francés,* where the number of pilgrims has risen and fallen in different periods but where there has always been at least a continuous trickle, the pilgrim route along the *Vía de la Plata* came to a complete halt for a long time, possibly for one or two centuries, and in the public eye, at least, it had disappeared into oblivion. It is was heavily promoted for the 2004 Holy Year, however, to attract pilgrims away from the completely saturated *Camino Francés* and there are plans afoot to classify the *Vía de la Plata* as *Patrimonio de Humanidad* as well.

The route is a varied one, in climate, scenery, history and architecture, and the pilgrim sees a big cross-section of Spain along it. The part from Seville to Astorga is not physically difficult to walk in that there are no stiff climbs but the distances between accommodation are still rather long in a few places. Once you enter Galicia, however, the route becomes very strenuous, with, for example, two passes (on two sucessive days) of over 1,200 m, though the pilgrim who has begun his or her journey in Seville will be fit by then and well able to tackle Galicia's constant climbs and descents. It is also a rather solitary route, which some people obviously like, but some of those who have done the *Vía de la Plata* after the *Camino* from Roncesvalles have said that they did not like it at all because they rarely met anyone else or any other pilgims, though this is gradually changing. The walking (or cycling) is almost all on old tracks and paths *(cañadas)*, very often the sort that are used for transporting animals or, if not, on extremely quiet minor roads. In Galicia much of the route is on old walled lanes (*correidoiras*). Otherwise the pilgrim is normally far away from roads, sometimes never seeing anybody at all, or any villages, all day long and it obviously needs a certain amount of organisation if you are not to get caught without anything to eat when you are hungry or short of water as there are very few public fountains along the way.)

How long does it take?

The walk from Seville to Santiago, whether via Astorga or Ourense, can be completed in six weeks by anyone who is fairly fit and who also likes to visit places of interest along the way. It can be undertaken in sections, too, by those who lack the time to do it all in one go or would just like to cover certain stretches, and indications are given in the text as to how to reach (or leave) the main towns along the way.

The route from Seville to Astorga is 722km (plus some 250km more along the *Camino Francés* for pilgrims who choose this alternative) while the route for those who go directly via Galicia to Santiago is 1000km so there is little difference between the two options, in terms of distance. People who "turn left" at Astorga often find it quite a shock, however, to be suddenly immersed in a sea of pilgrims after walking for so many weeks on their own or only with their companions and feel strangers amongst all the other pilgrims coming from the east who already know each other. The same applies, too, to those who continue through Galicia, and several pilgrims have commented that they found their arrival in Santiago somewhat depressing, particularly if they have already walked or ridden the *Camino francés*. (One suggestion made for dealing with this problem has been to continue on foot to Finisterre, using the three to four more days of walking as a quieter epilogue to your pilgrimage, akin to the often solitary character of the *Vía de la Plata*.)

Before you go

a) Read up as much as you can about the route, its history, art, architecture and geography. A short bibliography is given on page 8.

b) Do not expect anybody – anybody at all! – to speak English! You will have to communicate in Spanish all the time, for everything you need, however complicated, so if you are not already fairly fluent consider a year's evening classes or home study with tapes in your preparations: you will find it extremely difficult if you are unable to carry out practical transactions as well as feeling very isolated on what is already a solitary route if you are also unable to converse with the Spanish pilgrims and other people you meet along the way.

c) Decide what type of footwear you will be taking – for example, walking shoes, lightweight boots, heavy (thick-soled) trainers, and break them in before you go. Likewise, if you purchase a new rucksack for the journey, go out walking with it (fully laden) on as many occasions as you can before you set off.

Equipment

1. *Rucksack.* At least 50 litres if carrying a sleeping bag.
2. *Footwear* – both to walk in and a spare pair of lightweight trainers/sandals.
3. *Waterproofs..* A "poncho" (cape with a hood and space inside for a rucksack, preferably with front zip if walking alone as these are easier to put on single-handed) is far more useful (and far less hot) than a cagoule or anorak. (The disadvantage, of course, is that they can be very inconvenient in windy weather.)
4. *Pullover.* Much of the route is high up and as you go further north it can get cold at night, even in summer.
5. *First aid kit* (with needle for draining blisters). Adhesive dressings sold by the metre (e.g. Micropore). Scissors.
6. *High-factor sunscreen* if you burn easily.
7. *Large water bottle.* At *least* two litres (minimum) if walking in hot weather.
8. *Sleeping bag.* Essential if staying in refugios or other very basic accommodation.
9. *Sleeping mat.* Also essential for basic accommodation where you will have to sleep on the floor and useful for siestas in the open air.
10. *Stick.* Useful for frightening dogs and testing boggy terrain/depth of streams.
11. *Guidebook..*
12. *Maps.*
13. *Compass.*
14. *Torch.*
15. *Sun hat* (preferably with wide brim).
16. *Small dictionary.*
17. *Mug, spoon and knife.*
18. If you are addicted to tea/coffee or can't get going in the morning without a hot drink a *camping gaz* type stove is a great advantage, even though it will add extra weight to your luggage. This is especially useful in seasons when you will probably set out very early to avoid the heat, since although bars and cafés open early in Andalucía, the further north you go, the later they open, rarely before 8.30 or 9am except in big towns, and while in small places they may in fact be open many do not serve hot drinks until the early afternoon. (A few of the *refugios* that exist have cooking facilities but not all.) If you do take a *camping gaz* stove make sure it uses the 200g cylinders – smaller ones are not readily available in Spain. Alternatively, you could consider a "plunger" type electirc water boiler.
19. A *tent* is not worth the trouble as rooms are usually available (in bars, cafés) if you are not staying in the more basic accommodation, and campsites in Spain (of which there are few along the route anyway) can also be noisy and relatively expensive.

Pilgrim Records
Stamps for pilgrim passports

Modern pilgrims who seek proof of their pilgrimage also carry a *credencial* (pilgrim "passport") which they have stamped (with a *sello*) at regular intervals along the Way (such as churches, town halls, post offices) and which they then present to the cathedral authorities in Santiago to help them obtain their *compostela* or certificate of pilgrimage. More information about this is available from the Confraternity of St James or from the Cathedral in Seville (see page 10).

Bibliography

- María Cuenda and Darío Izquierdo, *La Virgen María en las Rutas Jacobeas. Ruta meridional – Vía de la Plata.* 1999. One of a set of three volumes (the other two deal with the *Camino francés* and the *Camino portugués*) that examine representations in art and architecture of the Virgin Mary along the *Vía de la Plata,* many of them linked with the theme and portrayals of St James. Contains excellent photographs.
- Salvador Llopis, *Por Salamanca también pasa el Camino de Santiago,* originally published in Salamanca in 1965 but reprinted in 1998 in Fuenterroble de Salvatierra by the Asociación de Amigos del Camino de Santiago "Vía de la Plata". As its title indicates, this book describes the route in the province of Salamanca, including variants.
- *La Ruta de la Plata, Camino mozárabe de Santiago,* Bilbao: Sua Edizoak, 1996. A guide to the route for motorists but with background information and photographs of interest to all types of pilgrim.
- *La Ruta de la Plata de Sevilla a Gijón,* León: Ediciones Lancia, 1993. Guide to the history of the route and its monuments, with good photographs.
- *La Ruta de la Plata: Guía práctica del viajero,* Madrid: Editorial Everest, 1994. Another guide to the route for motorists but with background material and photographs of interest to all types of pilgrim.
- José Sendín Blázquez, *Calzada y Camino de Santiago – Vía de la Plata – Historia, Mito, Leyenda,* Zamora: Fundación Ramos de Castro, 1992. As its title suggests, this is a collection of writings pertaining to the local history, myths and legends surrounding the southern route to Santiago.
- José Sendín Blázquez, *Mitos y leyendas del Camino de Santiago del Sur,* Plasencia: Ediciones Lancia, 1996. A further collection of history, myths and legends about people and places along the *Vía de la Plata.*

Guide Books

- *Guía del Camino Mozárabe de Santiago: Vía de la Plata,* Asociación de Amigos del Camino de Santiago Vía de la Plata, Seville: 2001, 174pp. ISBN: 84-931176-1-7. Covers both the route to Astorga and the one through Galicia, with good maps, details of accommodation and historical information relevant to the pilgrimage and a new edition is due in 2005. Available from the Asociación (see under heading *Useful Addresses* on page 10).
- *La Ruta de la Plata a Pie y en Bicicleta,* El País/Aguilar, 2000, 193pp, ISBN: 84-03-59537-9. Practical guide to the route but only from Mérida to Astorga. Repeats the *Camino Francés* section from Astorga to Santiago and completely omits all mention of the route from Seville to Mérida and from Zamora direct to Santiago through Galicia. Contains very good maps and information on the Roman aspects of the route (roads, bridges, history) but very little on the *Vía de la Plata* as a *pilgrimage* route.
- Joaquín Miguel Alonso, Juan Luis Rodríguez and Imagen MAS, *La Vía de la Plata,* León: Editorial Everest, 2004. Guide to the Vía de la Plata from Mérida to Astorga but describes the actual Roman road itself, not the *Camino de Santiago* as waymarked with yellow arrows, a pilgrim road which only follows in a general way the course of the original *calzada romana.*
- Ben Cole and Bethan Davies, *Walking the Vía de la Plata. The Camino de Santiago from Seville to Santiago de Compostela and on to Finisterre,* Vancouver: Pili Pala Press, 2004. Guide to the route from Seville to Santiago but does not describe either the

section from Granja de Moreruela to Astorga or include the 110 km waymarked southern option from A Gudiña to Ourense via Verín once the route enters Galicia. Good sketch maps, section on flora, fauna and birds but a book for hiking backpackers rather than an actual *pilgrim* guide.

- Alison Raju, *Way of St. James: Vía de la Plata,* Cicerone Press 2002, 220pp. ISBN: 1-85284-343-8. Covers the entire route (both options) with both historical and practical information (at present the only guide to the entire route in English).

Maps

Maps are a problem in Spain. To situate yourself generally, however (though not to walk from), three maps in the Michelin 1:400,000 (1cm to 4km) orange Regional Series are recommended: 578 Andalucía, 576 Extremadura and 571 Galicia. Such Spanish maps as are available in Britain can be purchased from, for example, Stanford's map shop (12 Long Acre, Covent Garden, London WC2 (020 7836-1321 or *www.stanfords.co.uk*), The Hereford Map Centre (01432 266322, e-mail: *mapped@globalnet.co.uk*), The Map Shop (15 High Street, Upton-upon-Severn, WR8 0HJ 9 (01684-593146 or *www.themapshop.co.uk*) which has a very efficient mail order service. or from some of the larger general bookshops.

Useful addresses

- Confraternity of St. James Tel: (020) 7928 9988
  27 Blackfriars Road, Web site: www.csj.org.uk
  London SE1 8NY E mail: office@csj.org.uk

- Amigos del Camino de Santiago de Sevilla: Vía de la Plata,
  Calle San Jacinto 25 Portal 6, Local 4,
  41010 Sevilla.
  Tel: 95 43.35.274 or 696 60.06.02
  Web site: viaplata.org.es
  E mail: sevilla@viaplata.org.es

- Asociación de Amigos del Camino de Santiago Vía de la Plata,
  Calle La Fuente 14,
  37769 Fuenterroble de Salvatierra,
  (Salamanca). Tel: 923.15.10.83

- Federación Asociaciones del Camino de Santiago Vía de la Plata
  Calle Santa Clara 33,
  49002 Zamora.

Web sites

As well as those listed above, all of which have links to other sites, you may find the following useful:

- www.caminomozarabe.com
- www.terra.es/personal6/caminomozarabe/etapas
- www.caminosantiago.org/cpperegrino/cpcaminos/caminomozarabe
- www.godescalco.com/iphp/etapas.php?via=plata

There and back
How to get there
Seville and Madrid: by air direct from London (the most practical option for cyclists) or Easyjet to Málaga, from where there is a frequent bus service to Seville; by train from London via Paris; by coach from London (change near Burgos). Seville can also be reached by bus from Madrid and other parts of Spain.

Other places along the Way (for those who are only doing a section) such as Mérida, Cáceres, Salamanca and Zamora are most easily reached by bus via Madrid. Salamanca can also be reached by train via Irún and Burgos.

How to get back from Santiago
Air: Rynair now has a service direct to Santiago from London (Stansted) but whether Iberia will continue their flights from Santiago to Heathrow is not yet known. (Check with them in their office in Santiago, though, about the continued availability of reduced flights homel on production of your *Compostela* - info. welcome.) Otherwise go to Madrid or Bilbao by coach or train and fly from there.

Train: to Paris. Leaves Santiago at 9am every day, arriving Hendaye late evening, in time for the connection overnight for Paris, arriving early the following morning. (If you want to break the journey, Irún - 5 mins before Hendaye - has much cheaper and more plentiful accommodation; take the *Topo* ("mole") train or walk to Hendaye the following morning.)

Coach: to Paris, direct, two to three times a week, depending on the time of year. Cheaper, comfortable and slightly shorter than the train journey, thougyh this now involves a change near Burgos. The journey takes 24 hours and arrives at the Porte de Bagnolet bus station from where you can buy a further ticket and continue to London. There is no longer a weekly service from Santiago to London in summer.

Finally, a very pleasant but slower way to return (and with more time to "come back down to earth") is to take the *FEVE* narrow-gauge railway along the north coast from El Ferrol via Oviedo to Santander. From there you can continue on the equally picturesque ET(a Basque narrow gauge railway company) via San Sebastián to Irún and from there take the *Topo* ("mole") train to Hendaye. You can get more information about this from the tourist office in Santiago (note that the FEVE is not part of the RENFE network). (Note, too, that the RENFE *regional* trains and the FEVE are more cyclist-friendly than the mainline *diurno* Talgo/Ave trains.)

Being there
Planning your schedule
As indicated, Seville to Santiago can be walked comfortably in six weeks by anyone who is fairly fit and who also likes to visit places of interest along the Way. Allow plenty of time when planning your itinerary, especially if you are not an experienced walker. Those starting in Seville and who are not experienced walkers or are not very fit have the advantage of being able to find accommodation at 20–25km stages, more or less as far as Mérida, so that by then, when you need to walk longer distances, you will already be fit and into the swing of things.

Try not to plan too tight a schedule but allow plenty of time and flexibility to account for unforeseen circumstances (pleasant or otherwise). Remember, too, that the weather on the *Vía de la Plata* is likely to be much hotter than on the *Camino Francés* - Cáceres, for example, frequently records temperatures as high as 50 degrees (centigrade). Where and how many rest days you take is up to you (though Seville, Mérida, Cáceres, Salamanca and Zamora are "musts" and a half day in Ourense is recommended), as is also whether you include several short days walking in your programme, arriving at your destination during the late morning so as to have the remainder of the day completely free. If you are extremely tired, though, or having trouble with your feet, a complete day off works wonders (particularly in a small place with no "sights" to be visited) and is well worth the seeming disruption to your schedule. Allow at least three days to visit Santiago at the end – there is plenty to see – and, especially if you continue via Astorga, you will meet up again with other pilgrims you encountered along the way.

Accommodation

Pilgrims who have already walked or cycled the *Camino Francés* will know that there are various types of accommodation available along the way, ranging from luxurious five-star hotels (such as the state-run *paradores* established in redundant historic buildings) down to very basic accommodation provided on the floor in community centres, former schools, sports halls and so on. Former pilgrims will also know that "hotel" usually implies a higher standard of accommodation than that found in a *hostal* which, in turn, normally offers more facilities than a *fonda, pensión* or a *casa huéspedes* (CH). (*Residencia* after either hotel or hostal means it only provides accommodation: neither meals nor breakfast are available.) There are also an increasing number of *Casas rurales* (CR) springing up along the way in country areas; these provide bead and breakfast, often an evening meal, but some of them have cooking facilities as well. (Do not confuse these establishments-moderately priced in the main - with a *Hotel rural* (HR), a newer category of accommodation whose meals, in particular, are often very expensive.) A number of bars also provide rooms (*habitaciones – camas* means 'beds') so it is worth asking about these, even if there is no sign or notice to say so. However, a word of warning if you intend to stay in any of these places and want to leave early in the morning to avoid walking in the heat: make sure you arrange to pay the previous evening and retrieve your passport as well as checking how you will actually get out of the building the following morning (which doors or entrances will be locked and how they can be opened), otherwise you may find yourself unable to leave until at least 9am. (Some pilgrims have suggested asking for rooms at the back of the building, or as high up as possible, in order to have a quieter night's rest.) Note too that you will find it difficult to find accommodation during the *Semana Santa* (the week before Easter Sunday), not only in places like Seville and Zamora, which are well known for these celebrations, but elsewhere as well. (It is also almost impossible to find anywhere to stay in Zafra and the surrounding area during the *feria* (agricultural fair), which lasts for the whole of September and the first week in October and public holidays such as October 12th - National Day - can also cause problems.) In general, the commercially available accommodation listed in this guide is at the middle to lower end of the market, especially where there is plenty of choice.

   Albergue turístico These establishments are part of a network set up by the Junta de Extremadura. They are not facilities exclusively for pilgrims (though they offer them a special rate) but also for individual and group tourists needing simpler accommodation. Note, however, that in smaller places without separate other facilities these *albergues* may also be used to house the itinerant homeless.

   Refugios, provided by churches, religious orders, *ayuntamientos* (town halls or local authorities) and some private individuals are increasingly being set up in different places along the *Via de la Plata* and there are now many such facilities. Note, however, that these establishments are **NOT** provided as cheap substitutes for hotels but as alternatives to sleeping rough, places to shelter pilgrims from the elements, so you cannot expect anything more than that they are clean and secure and that the facilities on offer work. Elsewhere there are places to sleep on the floor with basic washing facilities and these are indicated in the text as "R&F" (roof and floor), though in some cases they more offer more than just that. (Note, too, that unless you are quite sure that there is a "proper" refugio in the place in question, it is better to ask simply "is there somewhere for pilgrims to sleep?" Good spanish is usually needed to access some of these. In an emergency or as a last resort contact the local police or the *Protección Civil* (a combination of the ambulance and fire and rescue services in small places).

As indicated above, there are hardly any *campsites* along the *Vía de la Plata*.

Other practical information

Shops (for food) These can be found in most villages though in small places they may be unmarked and you will have to ask where they are (though in such places, bars often double up as shops). Make sure you always have adequate supplies of food in your rucksack, though, as on some parts of the route you won't pass any villages at all, all day long.

Bars Many bars along the *Vía de la Plata*, do not serve food or sandwiches, as they do on the *Camino Francés* (where a large proportion of their customers are pilgrims), unless they are a restaurant as well. The vast majority of people who frequent the bars on the *Vía de la Plata* are local - they eat at home and only go out to drink.

You will normally find at least one bar in every village you pass through, except in the very small ones in Galicia, though they may not always be marked and may not always serve hot drinks early in the day. You will, however, always find a bar in the *Hogar del Pensionista* (old people's club), in many sports' centres and swimming pools and in some *Casas consistoriales* and *Ayuntamientos* (townhalls) in smaller places.

Public holidays There are more of these (*días festivos*) than in Britain: January 1st, Good Friday, August 15th, October 12th, November 1st, December 5th, 6th and 25th. There are also three others which are taken locally and therefore vary from one area to another as well as (especially in August) the *fiestas* in honour of a town or village's own patron saint and which can last up to a week in some places. Shops, including those for food (but not usually bars or bakeries), will be closed on these occasions or open only in the mornings.

Water There are very few public fountains on the Seville - Astorga section of the *Vía de la Plata* but if left running permanently, these are usually safe to drink from (watch out for local people filling jugs and other containers at mealtimes as this tastes better than the chlorinated tapwater). *Agua (non) potable* means that it is (isn't) safe to drink and *agua non tratada* indicates that it is chlorine-free. Petrol stations on main roads are mentioned in the text as they usually sell cold drinks, chilled (bottled) water and, sometimes, limited food.

As well as carrying plenty of water with you make sure you drink plenty as well. It is difficult to do but in hot weather try to drink at least half a litre (or more) when you get up in the morning, as well as any tea/coffee you may have as in this way you will be less likely to become dehydrated. Keep drinking at regular intervals, even if you don't think you are thirsty because if you *do* become dehydrated it will then be too late to do anything about it quickly enough, even if you have supplies with you. The best cure, when available, is large quantities of very hot drinks (e.g. herbal tea) and a lengthy bath/shower.

Poste restante If you want to send things to yourself further along the route (such as maps and guides) or have people write to you, you can do this via the *poste restante* system whereby you collect your mail (on presentation of your passport) at the post office. This service is called *Lista de Correos* in Spain, is free, and items are kept for you for a month before returning them to the sender. Address the letter/parcel to yourself, *Lista de Correos*, postal code and name of town and province. (The most likely places you will need will be 41080 Sevilla, 06080 Mérida, 10080 Cáceres, 37080 Salamanca, 49080 Zamora, 32080 Ourense and 15780 Santiago de Compostela.) If you decide (while in Spain) that you have too much in your rucksack it is considerably cheaper to post it to yourself this way to Santiago than to send a parcel home to Britain. Make sure, however, when collecting such items, that the clerk looks not only under your surname (*apellido*) but also under your first name (*nombre*); as the Spanish system of surnames is different you may find your mail has been filed in the wrong place.

Telephones In Spain (which has one of the most expensive telephone systems in Europe) phone boxes usually take both coins as well as phone cards (*tarjeta telefónica*, available in newsagents). Most Spanish area codes begin with a 9, which is included when calling from abroad, and numbers beginning with a 6 are mobile phones. The emergency number for the *Guardia Civil* is 062. Telephone books (*guía telefonica*) are by province (white and yellow pages in separate books) and entries are then arranged by *town* or *population centre* so that it is easy to locate, for example, hotels and *fondas* in a specific place. Postcodes are also included.

Internet cafés can be found in all main towns along the route - Sevilla, Mérida, Cáceres, Salamanca, Zamora, Ourense - but as the locations of these faciloities often change it is better to enquire in the Tourist Office in the place concerned.

Dogs live all along the route from Seville to Santiago, usually running around loose, hear you ages before you have any idea where they are and are often enormous (though the small ones are, in fact, a greater nuisance, as they have a nasty habit of letting you pass quietly by and then attacking from behind, nipping you in the back of your ankles). A stick is very useful, even though you might not normally want to walk with one – not to hit them with but to threaten. When you do meet them keep on walking at a steady pace (do not run, under any circumstances) and if you see flocks of sheep or goats apparently alone give them a very wide berth as they will be accompanied if not by two then certainly by their four-legged guardians.

Fording streams If you come to a river/stream with no bridge and no stepping stones you will have to wade across. This is not a very common occurrence but if you do need to, remember to keep your shoes/boots on or wear sandals as you may not always be able to see sharp objects or detect how clean the water is. You are also less likely to over balance than you might be with a heavy rucksack and bare feet.

Stamps for pilgrim passports (*sello*) are becoming easier to obtain than they used to be - from churches, *ayuntamientos*, the local police, the post office and *refugios* where they exist.

Church services Masses are normally held at 8pm in places of any size, as well as the usual Sunday morning and Saturday evening services. However, the *Vía de la Plata* differs from the *Camino Francés* in another respect too, for the time being, at least, in that there are no specially pilgrim masses in churches along the way or pilgrim prayers held in refugios. Those passing through or starting in Roncesvalles, for example, have the opportunity to receive a pilgrim blessing before continuing/beginning their journey but there is no such possibility in Seville at present, either in the cathedral itself or in any other church in that city either. The only place on the *Vía de la Plata* where specifically pilgrim services are organised, when numbers warrant it, is in Fiuenterroble de Salvatierra.

Spectacles If you wear glasses it may be a good idea to carry a spare pair or at least your prescription with you in case you lose/break them.

Prices have not been given in each individual entry but, in general, in 2004, a set-price *menu del día* cost between 6 and 9 euros and a single room between 10 and 18 euros per night in a basic *hostal* or *pensión*.

Using this guide
Waymarking

The route given in this book starts at the cathedral in Seville and is waymarked in one direction only. Those who would like to walk the route in reverse or return on foot will therefore find it extremely difficult, although the white waymarking in reverse, mentioned below, will help. Waymarking *(señalización)* is in the form of yellow arrows *(flechas)*, familiar to those who have walked the *Camino Francés*, painted on tree trunks, walls, road signs, rocks, the ground, sides of buildings and so on, and are normally extremely easy to spot. They appear at frequent intervals and the walker will not usually encounter any difficulty following them. Note, however, that with the exception of Seville, La Bañeza and Ourense, the waymarking in cities and other urban areas is often non-existent or leaves a great deal to be desired.

The Seville–Astorga section has also been used, in reverse, from Gijón to Cáceres, as a *ruta de transhumancia*, used for droving animals in large numbers, and in 1995 the practice was revived and huge numbers of cattle were moved on foot to try and help restore the tradition. Anybody walking the route who sees white waymarking in reverse (somewhat patchy in places) may have wondered what these white arrows were for: they were painted to guide the people driving cattle.

Textual description

Each section begins with the distance walked from the previous one, the height above sea-level where known, the cumulative distance covered already and the distance left to Santiago via Ourense on the northern option through Laza; for the route that continues from Granja de Moreruela to Astorga only the distance already covered is given, whilst on the southern variant through Galicia only the kilometres from place to place are indicated. This is followed by a description of the facilities available in each town or village, a brief history, where applicable, and an indication of the places of interest to visit. (Pilgrims wishing to spend time in any of the larger towns should obtain information leaflets and a street plan from the tourist office there.) The text is not divided up into stages as in this way the walker (or cyclist) can decide for him or herself the distances he or she would like to cover each day. The figures after each placename heading indicate the height in metres where known

Abbreviations

LH = left hand, RH = right hand, rte = restaurante, YH = youth hostel, CD = cash dispenser, km = kilometre, pp. = per person, CRS = cycle repair shop, RENFE is the abbreviation for the Spanish national railway network, s/n after a street name in an address means *sin número* (establishment in question does not have a number, either because the street is very short or because the building − bank, museum, big hotel, for example − is extremely large).

When to go? The route is practicable, though not necessarily recommended, all through the year (and definitely *not* in July and August if you are starting in Seville, when the temperatures will be well up into the high nineties Fahrenheit and beyond). In winter the days are short, it is often very windy on the southern part of the route and it rains a lot in Galicia. The weather may be dry over much of the route through Extremadura and Castille and León but as a lot of it is quite high up (Salamanca, for instance, is at over 760m though the area around it is more or less flat) it gets very cold, with a biting wind. If you are not restricted to a particular time of year, the end of April to the middle of June or the autumn are best − dry, but not as hot as in summer, and accommodation is also much less crowded (see note in the *Accommodation* section for periods to avoid.) Remember, too, that if you start from Seville too early in September it will still be very hot and that by he time you reach Galicia it may well be cold and *extremely* wet!

Slides If you have the foresight at the time, consider taking *two* pictures of topics that you think would be useful to add to the CSJ's slide library.
    It is recommended, however, that you do *not* send unprocessed film back home while you are away. The X-ray equipment that now forms part of the increasingly sophisticated security systems established in airports and on arrival in Dover/Calais, for example, may permanently damage your unprocessed film. (The hand-baggage X-rays are reported to be film-friendly, though.)

Feedback This guide, like the others produced by the CSJ, can only be kept as up-to-date as possible with the help of its users, who are invited to report their experiences, both good and bad, to the editor (address inside back cover), so that future editions can be suitably amended.

* * * * * * *

Finally, for pilgrims who attend mass and who would like to be able to join in at least once during the service the Lord's Prayer is given below in Spanish:

Padre nuestro, que estás en el cielo,
santificado sea tu Nombre;
venga a nosotros tu reino;
hágase tu voluntad en la tierra como en el cielo.
Danos hoy nuestro pan de cada día;
perdona nuestras ofensas,
como también nosotros perdonamos
a los que nos ofenden;
no nos dejes caer en la tentación,
y líbranos del mal.

Puebla de Sanabria , Iglesia de Santa María del Azogue

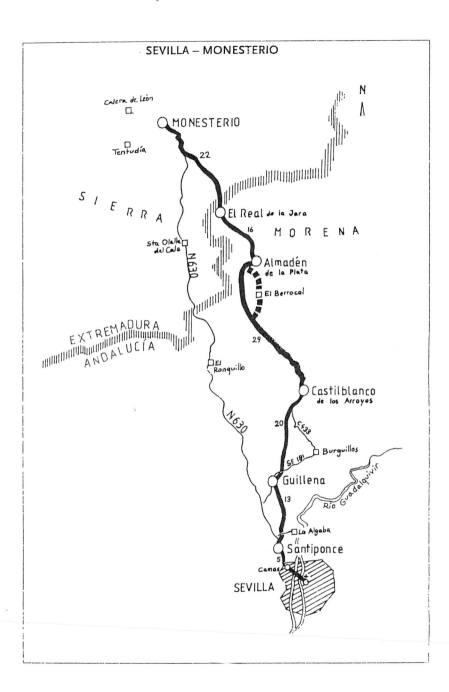

THE ROUTE

Seville 12m, 650,000 (0/1000)

The fourth-largest city in Spain, the Hispalis of Roman times, situated on the Río Guadalquivir. All facilities; international airport, RENFE, buses to all parts of Spain. Accommodation in all price brackets but no *refugio* or specifically pilgrim accommodation. Tourist Office at Avenida de la Constitución 21.

As indicated in the Introduction the Asociación de Amigos del Camino de Santiago issue special *Vía de la Plata credenciales* ("pilgrim passports", address on page 10). You can also obtain one (and the first stamp for this "passport") from the cathedral office, entering by the Puerta de la Campanilla, 11-14 hrs and 16-19 hrs, Monday to Friday only.

Try to spend at least one whole day here. The major monuments include the cathedral, the Giralda, the alcázar and gardens, Pilate's House, the Santa Cruz quarter. The best way to see Seville is on foot (ask at tourist office for map with walking tour and for details of combined ticket giving entry to principal monuments). Santiago and pilgrim-related references include a painting of St James (by Juan de Roelas) in Capilla de Santiago in Cathedral Santa María de la Sede (north aisle), statue of San Roque in chapel of Hospital de la Caridad and statue of St James the Pilgrim in a niche adjacent to the frame of the cathedral's west portal).

A word of warning: Seville is notorious for its thieves and pickpockets.

On your first day there are two possibilities:

a) you can walk from Seville to Santiponce (10km) in the late afternoon/early evening, with time to visit the Roman city of Italica (check first with Tourist Office re. closing day) without your rucksack and then return by bus (half-hourly or more frequent service in the week, hourly on Sundays) to Seville (*Plaza de Armas* bus station, by river) to sleep. This section is very industrial, not very scenic, and this option would enable you to walk on to Castilblanco de los Arroyos (33km from Seville) the following day.

b) you can leave Seville in the morning and walk to Guillena (23km), a short day with time to visit Italica en route.

The route starts from the cathedral and you will find the first yellow arrow on a lampost on the pavment opposite the statue of Santiago Peregrino on the west front of the building. After crossing the river Guadalquivir there are two options, one along the riverside, the other via Camas; the latter is very built up but is useful in bad weather when the low-lying area by the river may be flooded.

5km Camas 13m (5/995)
Shops, bars, bank, etc. Hostal El Cruce. Hostal El Madera is midway between Camas and Santiponce.

5km Santiponce 16m (10/990)
Shops, bars, bank (+CD), Hotel Ventorillo Canario opposite entrance to Italica.

Site of Roman city of Italica, founded in AD 206, with Roman theatre on outskirts (city buses from Seville terminate here). Reported free entrance to EU citizens (info. welcome). Monasterio de San Isidoro has now been restored and visits possible.

13km Guillena 22m (23/977)
All facilities, hotel Hostal/Bar Francés has rooms (tel: 955.78.51.77) and does meals. Ask at *Policía local* for PS and for R&F in sports centre (make sure you have the key to enter the little door at night).

15th c. church of Nuestra Señora de la Granada.

3km Venta la Casa de Pradera (26/974) Bar/mesón (open early).

16km Castilblanco de los Arroyos 329m (42/958)

Small town with all facilities. *Refugio* located behind petrol station on main road at entrance to village (ask attendant for key and PS: only 6 beds but plenty of floor space, hot showers). Hotel Castilblanco (at entrance to town, tel: 954.73.48.11), Pensión Salvadora (unmarked, 43 Avenida España,tel: 955 73.45.09). Bar Isidoro, Avenida de la Paz, does food, as does Bar Reina on main road.

16th c. Iglesia del Divino Salvador.

16km El Berrocal (58/942) *A provincial nature reserve, dedicated to replanting of trees.*

The *Camino* (waymarked with usual yellow arrows) takes you through 13km of undulating woods, with no prominent features apart from three ruined houses though several herds of deer are visible if you are attentive. However, the "reward" comes at the end when, after climbing a very steep hill, you suddenly arrive at the

11km Miradores del Cerro del Calvario 550m (69/931)

Two viewpoints, like brick pulpits, with plunging view of Almadén de la Plata and the blue marble quarries (of Roman origin) to the north and the Sierra del Norte de Sevilla (that you have just come through) to the south. Splendid views in all directions. Cerro del Calvario was also, formerly, a place of religious cult.

Cyclists, however, may prefer to continue on the road to Almadén de la Plata; the ride through El Berrocal is very quiet and pleasant, most of it on easily rideable tracks, but for the last kilometre up to the two *miradores* you will have to get off and push your bike *very* steeply uphill. The view from the top is probably worth it though the descent the other side (1.5km) is also steep and you will need to walk part of the way down too. Alternatively, if you feel like walking up to see the view you can do so from Almadén – the path is signposted from the town.

1.5km Almadén de la Plata 449m (70.5/929.5)

Small town with all facilities. New 76 bed *refugio*/youth hostel on *Camino* on way out of town (6e, bunks, sheets): ask in *ayuntamiento.* or Oficina de Turismo (opposite church) for key and also PS or phone 954.73.50.25. or 625.41.00.00. Bar Casa Concha (tel: 954 73.50.43, 12e single) and Bar Las Macias (tel: 954.73.54.61) both have rooms.

Church of Nuestra Señora de Gracia. The ayuntamiento, with its clocktower, was built in early 20th century behind façade of the former Ermita de Nuestra Señora de los Angeles. Here, as in many other small towns in the south, (bitter) orange trees line the streets, much as plane trees do in Britain and France. Almadén formerly had a church dedicated to Santiago.

From here you have two options. You can either continue all the way to El Real de la Jara on a quiet, undulating and fairly shady road with little traffic (cyclists will find this an easier alternative) or go on paths, very hilly but with spectacular scenery, through the Cortijo Arroyo Mateos, a private estate; the route is well waymarked and it is no longer necessary to telephone the estate office the evening before as the gates are now opened every morning and you can both enter and leave without any problem).

On the minor road before entering El Real on the second option, at KM1, there is a memorial to the late José Luis Salvador Savador (the founder of the Seville Amigos) where part of his ashes are buried; the rest are in the outside wall of the refugio in Fuenterroble de Salvatierra (Salamanca).

16.5km El Real de la Jara 460m (87/913)
Small town with all facilities (bank+CD). New private refugio reported: is this the same as the unmarked *pensión (Casa Concha)* at no. 70 on main road *(Calle Real)*? Info.welcome. R&F: pilgrims with *credenciales* can sleep in the changng rooms in the Campo de Futbol, almost 1km out of town on the main road: contact the Oficina de Turismo on the first floor of the *ayuntamiento* to arrange to have the key, also for PS.

12km Ermita de San Isidoro (99/901)
You have now left the province of Sevilla and the autonomous region of Andalucía (shortly after El Real) and have entered the province of Badajoz in the autonomous región of Extremadura.

Note: in this area there are also other waymarked long-distance walks (with yellow *and white* markers). Be careful not to follow these as only in places (not all the time) do they coincide with those of the *Vía de la Plata.* Similarly "VP" signs refer not to the *Vía de la Plata* but to the *Vía Pecuaria,* a route waymarked in white from Almadén to Monesterio

Chapel on site where the retinue transporting the body of San Isidoro up the Vía de la Plata from Seville to León stopped en route to his final resting place in the Basilica de San Isidoro in León. After this the landscape begins to change, the cortijos (very large estates) disappear and there are a lot of walled lanes. You will also see many donkeys in this area, still used to work the land.

8km Cruz del Puerto 753m (107/893) Large picnic area, wayside shrine, fountain (but not always working).

1km Monesterio 752m (108/892)
Small town with all facilities (bank+CD) and plenty of accommodation of all types, including Hostal D.P. El Pilar on main road (tel: 941.51.67.56). Small *refugio* for those with *credencial* at former Cruz Roja on LH side of main road at entry to town (key and PS from Hotel Moya next door, which has pilgrim menu).

Two side trips (on foot or bicycle) are recommended from here:

a) 7km west of here, at Calera de León, there is the medieval monastery of the Order of Santiago, with Gothic church and two-storied cloister (worth visiting). You can walk there by deviating from the Camino. Leave the town as normal but then follow the yellow **and white** *markers which will lead you all the way there (shop, bars). To return to the Vía de la Plata (not waymarked) take the local road (signposted "N630 6km") for 3km. At the top of the hill turn L at the third white gate posts with cattle grid (wide track with no gates on RH side of road here).: this is the point where the camino crosses the local road.*

b) 8km to the monastery of Tentudía is also recommended. (The name is a corruption of "hold the day," as the Virgin Mary extended the daylight so that the Christians could complete their defeat of the Moors here.) It contains the courtyard of a mosque, Mozarabic, Mudéjar, late Romanesque and Classical elements, a Capilla de Santiago and fine Italian tile-work, including a splendid tile Santiago Matamoros in the chapel. Open 10.15hrs to 5.25hrs, free, closed Mondays. To walk there from Monesterio follow the

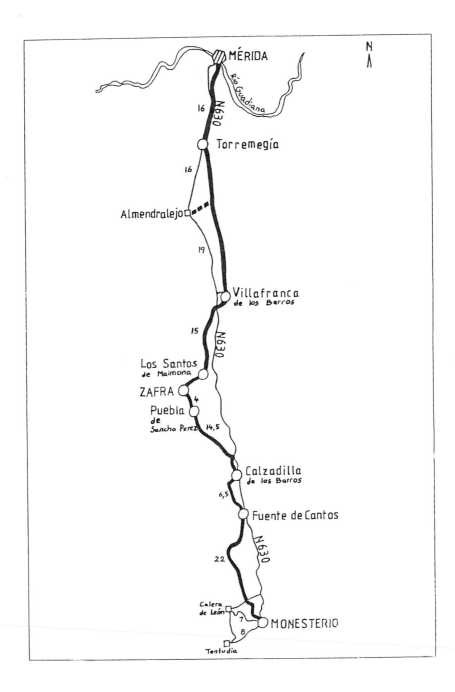

signs to Calera de León and Tentudía west off the N630 up Calle Primero de Mayo and Avenida Ramón y Cajal. *500m beyond the modern Ermita de Nuestra Señora de Tentudía turn R along waymarked path (yellow and white flashes) for 8km to monastery. Retrace your steps for the return journey.*

Note: There is hardly any shade, no water and no villages between Monesterio and Fuente de Cantos.

22km Fuente de Cantos 583m (130/870)

Small town with all facilities. Casa Vicente on main road (tel: 924.50.02.77) has rooms. Hotel La Fábrica in converted flour mill at end of town close to main road (tel: 924.50.00.42) reported good but is more expensive

New *Albergue de Turismo,* very quiet and calm, in a converted convent on outskirts of town (15e incl. filling beakfast). To go there: from *Plaza de la Constitución* (with back to *ayuntamiento)* pass to L of church and turn 1st L down *Calle Arias Montano* to bottom and then continue on *Calle de los Frailes* (ask for "Casa Rural"). R&F? Info.welcome.

One of the town's two churches is another Iglesia de Nuestra Señora de la Granada, containing a) statue of Santiago Apóstol on main altar (with shells on each lapel) and b) statue of San Roque on RH side of church (when facing altar). Fuente de Cantos was also the birthplace of the painter Zurbarán (the Casa can be visited).

Note: There is no shade at all between here and Zafra.

6.5km Calzadilla de los Barros 556m (136.5/863.5)

Shops, bars, farmacia, bank. YH with kitchen (but no cooker, 1.7km away, ask at *ayuntamiento* for key). Hostal Rodríguez (on N630, tel: 924.58.47.01) reported cheap and basic.

Large ceramic tile plaque on wall at entry, with map and indication of the town's monuments. These include the 16th c. Ermita de Nuestra Señora de la Encarnación, the Ermita de San Isidro and the fortress-style parish church of the Divino Salvador (14th to 16th c.); this is a National Monument, as is also its main altarpiece (15th to 16th c.) by Antón de Madrid, with 23 sections depicting scenes from the life of Christ. Town coat of arms contains scallop shell and sword of Santiago.

15km Puebla de Sancho Pérez 522m (151.5/848.5)

Three shops (one at entry on L), bars (though all seem to shut down in the afternoons except Bar Galea on main road at end of village).

Iglesia de Santa Lucía, Ermita de Nuestra Señora de Belén.

4.5km Zafra 509m pop. 15,000 (156/844)

All facilities, RENFE, buses to Madrid, Seville, Mérida, Salamanca and other parts of Spain. Tourist Office in the Plaza de España.

Albergue turístico reported, 22 beds, on L at beginning Calle Ancha (near old town). Hostal Carmen, Avenida de la Estación 9, has two restaurants (Rogelio and Nuevo Rogelio) and rooms (tel: 924.55.14.39). Hostal Arias (tel: 924.55.48.55) by petrol station on the Badajoz road (200m off *camino*), Hostal Las Palmeras in Plaza Grande (reported good value) plus several others. For pilgrim stamp and spartan *refugio* facility (reported closed for building works - info. welcome) organised by the "Amigos" in Zafra (but not available during September or early October) ask at *Policía local* in centre of town.

Warning: as indicated in the Introduction, during the Feria de Zafra (agricultural fair)

which takes place during the whole of September and the first week in October it will be *impossible* to find anywhere to stay, either in Zafra or in the *pensión* in Los Santos de Maimona. During this period it is suggested (pilgrims with *credencial* only, however) that you continue to Los Santos and sleep in the *albergue juvenil* there (access via *Policía Local* in *Casas Consistoriales*).

Zafra is a historic town (often described as a "mini Seville" with castle of the Dukes of Feria (now a parador), Colegiata de Nuestra Señora de la Candelaria (contains an altarpiece with painted panels by Zurbarán in a south lateral chapel and a Santiago Apóstol on main Baroque altarpiece; church is kept locked except at service times so best time to visit is just before evening mass). Former Hospital de Santiago still standing.

5km Los Santos de Maimona 528m, pop. 8,100
Shops, bars, banks. Pensión Sanse II (tel: 924.54.42.10) near main road at far end of town. *Albergue juvenil* (youth hostel, with bunks, kitchen) accessible via *Policía local* (who also have pilgrim stamp) in *Casas Consistoriales* (tel: 924.54.42.94 if closed).

Maimona was a Moorish king and the "Santos" not saints but merely "altos", high-placed, important people, and there are several large historic houses in the town. The building which is now the town hall ("Casas Consistoriales") was once the Palacio de la Encomienda (Command HQ) of the Order of the Knights of Santiago and Los Santos formerly had a pilgrim hospital as well. Municipal coat of arms has cross of Santiago and two scallop shells and church has a Puerta del Perdón (where pilgrims who were too weak or ill to continue were granted the same remission of their sins and the same indulgences as those who completed the journey to Santiago; lion with sword of Santiago above door).

15.5km Villafranca de los Barros 450m pop.12,600
Small town with all facilities. New *albergue turístico* "La Almazara" (tel: 686.89.88.410) at KM670 on the N630 on edge of town, in a former oil mill. Special pilgrim price (12 € incl. bkft). Hostal Horizonte (tel: 924.52.56.99, not open all year), Pensión Mancera Lara (reports vary), Bar/Rte La Marina (corner of Avenida F. Aranguén and N630) has rooms, Hotel Diana, Casa Chica 29 (reported good value), Casa Perín, Calle Caillo Arias 40 (tel; 924.52.53.56, 18e pp.), Hotel Romero 1km away on main road. PS in *ayuntamiento.*

Church of Santa María (much shell decoration inside, San Roque in south porch and Santiago Apóstol with book and shell in main altarpiece) and a number of interesting old houses.

17.5km Almendralejo 337m, pop. 23,600 (194/806)
Medium-sized town with all facilities, wine production centre. Bar Hotel Los Angeles* (on main road), Hotel España** (turn R after reaching main road in town, reported good value and friendly), and several new modern hotels (expensive) on main road to L on entering town,several restaurants. Is R&F still available at Caritas' *albergue para transeuntes* (2km away in centre of town)? Info. welcome.

If you stay in Almendralejo you can either return to detour point before continuing or rejoin the *camino* (turning L onto it) 3km to north by taking road to Alange marked "Don Benito" at crossing on leaving town.

The town itself is not on the Vía de la Plata as it dates only from 1536 and was therefore not on the calzada romana. *Ermita de Santiago (in outer suburb, 2km to west).*

10.5km Torremegía 302m (204.5/795.5)
Shops, bars, rte. Hotel now closed, but an albergue turístico reported next to church, at end of *Calle Grande* (a converted palace with 20 beds, rte, bar, 12 €). PS in Casa Consistorial.
Iglesia de la Concepción, Palacio de los Megía (with shells surrounding the door).

16km Mérida 218m, 51,600 (220.5/779.5)
All facilities, RENFE, buses to Madrid, Seville, Cáceres, Salamanca. Capital of the autonomous region of Extremadura. No pilgrim-only accommodation but hotels and hostales include Hostal Senero (Calle Holguín 12, tel: 924.31.72.07, also has PS), Hostal Nueva España (Avenida de Extremadura 6, tel: 924.31.33.56), Hostal Anas (Avenida Reina Sofía 9, tel: 924.31.11.13) and Pensión Alameda, Calle Magdalena 1 (tel: 924.30.04.74, on outskirts near San Lázaro acqueduct). Tourist Office: Calle Saenz de Burnaga s/n (near Roman theatre). PS: *Ayuntamento.*
Mérida was founded in 23 BC as a settlement for veterans of the Iberian wars (hence its name: Augusta Emerita). It contains more important remains of Roman antiquity than any other town in Spain and it is worth spending a whole day here. Roman amphitheatre, theatre (still used), bridge over the River Guadiana (one of the longest of its kind), National Museum of Roman Art (reported free to pilgrims, info.welcome), Visigothic Museum (free), Trajan's Arch, Alcazaba, church of Santa Eulalia (the city's patron), church of Santa María. Note, however, that to visit the major Roman and Christian monuments you have to buy a combined ticket for all of them (reduction for over 60's) though you do not need to visit them all on the same day; individual tickets are not available.

7km Embalse de Proserpina (227.5/772.5)
Now a tourist attraction with water sports, several cafés (not open early), *chiringuitos* (open-air snack bars), restaurant and campsite (open April 1st to September 15th). *The reservoir supplied Mérida with its drinking and other water in Roman times.*

7.5km El Carrascalejo 308m (235/765)
Fountain but no other facilities of any kind. *Church of Nuestra Señora de la Consolación.*

2.5km Aljucén 270m (237.5/762.50)
Two bars, shop, farmacia, fountain. Municipal *refugio* run for the village by Elena Martínez & Ana Josefa Cazoría, who also have a *Casa Rural* at Calle San Andrés 23 (tel: 924.31.28.23), B&B, eve. meal, reported very friendly.
Church of San Andrés has Santiago crosses on all its pedestals (inside the building).
Between here and Alcuéscar you leave the province of Badajoz and enter that of Cáceres. For the next 15km you will not pass a single building and are unlikely to meet anyone at all. This section is well-enough waymarked but watch out carefully for the yellow arrows as the route is not always as straightforward as you might expect. Like many other areas of the *Vía de la Plata,* this one is a paradise of wild flowers in the springtime.
Make sure you have enough water before you leave Aljucén.

15.5km Cruz de San Juan/Cruz del Niño Muerto (253/747)
Stone wayside cross, so named because on one such feast day (June 24th, Midsummer's

MÉRIDA – CÁCERES

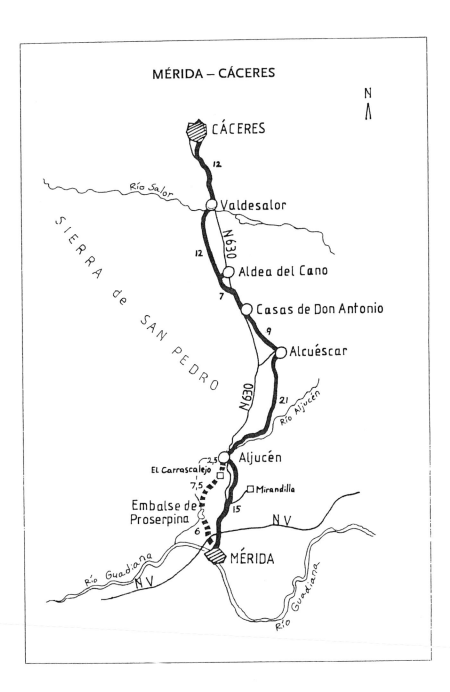

Day, celebrating the anniversary of St John the Baptist) a young shepherd boy coming to the fiesta from the Valle de la Zarza was eaten by a wolf.

6km Alcuéscar 489m (259/741)

Shops, bars. Casa Alejandro in upper part of village and Bar El Trio lower down both do meals. Accommodation (for pilgrims with *credencial* only) and PS at the Residencia for handicapped men run by the Hermanos Esclavos de María y de los Pobres at the bottom of the village on the way out. (Note, however, that although they do not charge you should leave a donation.) Hostal Canuto, Hostal Los Olivos and Hotel Residencia Cruz de las Herrerías are located at KM249 on the N630 at the junction with the local road to Alcuéscar, 3km to west.

If you would like to visit the isolated Visigothic church of Santa Lucía de Trampal (east of Alcuéscar) you can do so by following the well-signed track, out of the Plaza de España in Alcuéscar, 2.5km each way.

10km Casas de Don Antonio 413m (269/731)

Bar in village and another on N630 at exit. No accommodation.

Ermita de la Virgen del Pilar (with relief statute of Santiago Apóstol on altarpiece and statue of Santiago Matamoros) at exit.

7km Aldea del Cano 396m (276/724)

Fountain, shops, bars in centre of village on other side of road. Bar/rte "Las Vegas" on N630 (which also has the key for very basic *refugio* accommodation in the school nearby: no beds but hot showers). Casa Rural reported - info. welcome. *Church of San Martín.*

11km Valdesalor 380m (287/713)

Shop, bars, bar/rte by petrol station (closed Mon.?) PS in *ayuntamiento* (where R&F with hot showers also reported available: ask for key in *Hogar del Pensionista*). *Church of San Pedro.*

12km Cáceres 464m, pop. 69,193 (299/701)

All facilities, RENFE, buses to Madrid and places along the Gijón–Seville service. Accommodation in all price brackets, including Hostal Almonte (Calle Gil Cordero 6, tel: 927.24.09.25) and Pensión Carretero (Plaza Mayor 22, tel: 927.24.74.82) but no pilgrim-only facilities. New *albergue turístico* near centre of old town (Calle Margallo 36, tel: 630.50.41.95, 40pl., 20e incl. bkft, kitchen?) Municipal *albergue turístico* also reported in Avenida de la Universalidad (52 beds): from Plaza Mayor goes down Calle Muñoz then Avenida San Blas to park to R. Tourist Office: Plaza Mayor 33. CRS: Bicicletas Cáceres, Calle de Badajoz 10. PS in *ayuntamiento* (entrance at rear).

City founded in Roman times with the old town, dating from the 13th century onwards, completely self-contained within the modern one. Surrounded by its walls with gates and towers, it has many monuments worth visiting, whether churches, palaces or other imposing houses (two-hour guided walking tour of the historic quarter available from tourist office in the mornings). Church of Santiago (just outside the old city centre, like those in Salamanca and Zamora, and as was often customary for pilgrim churches) has a bas-relief of a pilgrim with staff, scrip, hat and shell and a Santiago Matamoros in the main

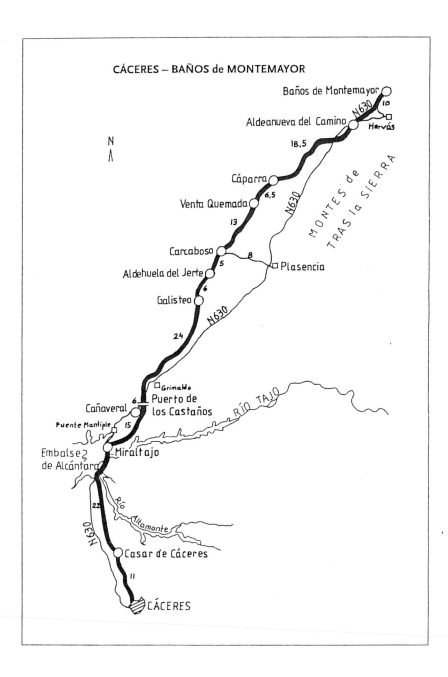

CÁCERES – BAÑOS de MONTEMAYOR

altarpiece *(see central insert for other Santiago references in Cáceres). Another place worth spending a whole day.*

11km Casar de Cáceres 369m (310/690)
Shops, bars, bank. Good *refugio* in square opposite the *ayuntamiento* (20 beds, showers, kitchen; key from bar of Rte Majuca (next to *Policía local*). PS in *ayuntamiento*. Hostal Las Encinas 3km away on N630, near KM542 (tel: 927. 29.02.01) but if you stay here you will have to return to the village to continue on the *camino*, picking up arrows again near the Ermita de Santiago (north of the village).

Iglesia de la Asunción (parish church, in centre of village) has a Baroque wood painted Santiago on LH side of main altarpiece with fine Santiago Peregrino complete with staff, gourd, hat and scallop and modern but inverted black scallop in grille of SW chapel. The town also has four ermitas, one each to its north, south, east and west; Santiago, to the north, has modern Santiago Matamoros with a giant sword above the altar while those to the south, east and west are dedicated, respectively, to San Bartolomé, Los Mártires and La Soledad.

(Over to your L, before you reach the former hostal, *you can see the* Embalse de Alcántara *(reservoir) and the* Torreón de Floripes, *the only remains of the village of Alconétar after it was flooded to make the reservoir.)*

> Note: 3km after crossing the *Río Almonte* you pass the *Apeadero del Río Tajo* (a railway halt). If you are very tired or the weather is atrocious you may like to know that there is one train a day (7 days a week) from here to Cañaveral (on the Madrid-Badajoz line); it leaves Cáceres at 14.30, passes the halt at 14.50 and arrives in Cañaveral at 15.07.

Otherwise, after crossing the *Río Tajo* it is 1.5km to the (now closed)

20km Hostal Miraltajo 250m (330/670)
Closed and up for sale since late 2003. *Albergue turístico* near reservoir, not far from hostal but need to phone ahead for it to be opened (check with Tourist Office in Cáceres beforehand?) Info. welcome.

Pilgrims interested in Roman bridges may like to make a 4km detour from here to the huge, imposing Puente Mantible/Puente Alconétar which was re-sited in a valley beside the N630 when the reservoir flooded its original position. Take the gravel path to the north end of the Hostal terrace and follow it down to the banks of the reservoir and then nearly all the way to the bridge: you may need to scramble up to the N630 for a short distance to avoid cliffs.

14km Cañaveral 362m, pop. 2100 (344/656)
Bars, shops, bank (+CD). Small refugio (4-6pl.) in old house in centre of town (mixed reports) - ask in *ayuntamiento.* (New larger facilities reported planned for another location.) Hostal/Rte Málaga (tel: 927.30.00.67) on main road. RENFE *apeadero* (railway halt) 1km out of town.

14th to 16th c.Iglesia de Santa María, 16th c. Ermita de San Roque.

2km Ermita de San Cristóbal (346/654)

4km Puerto de los Castaños 500m (350/650)
No facilities at all.

The next section (as far as Galisteo) is **NOT** suitable for *cyclists*, even on mountain bikes. They should continue on the main road for 3km more, until just after *Grimaldo* (bar) and then turn L on a minor road to Holguero. KSO at a crossroads with the Torrejoncillo–Riolobos road and then turn R at the next crossroads along another minor road more or less following the Río Alagón to Galisteo.

Walkers: FP is signposted off route to *"Grimaldo, 500m"* (bar, castillo, 10km from Cañaveral). Small *refugio* (8-10 beds, kitchen?) in schoolhouse (ask in bar, which also does meals and has PS).

22km Galisteo 308m (372/628)
Small town with shops, bars, bank, *Hogar del Pensionista* in main square does simple food. Bar/Rte "Los Emigrantes" at entrance does meals and has rooms (special rate for pilgrims? Info.welcome.) 2 *refugios*: a) municipal, in building by campsite, by river on leaving town but key from Pedro Serrano, 5 Plaza de España (in centre of town); b) private *refugio* 14 pl., basic kitchen, 6e) run by Mesón Rusticiana (which also does meals - reported good: turn L at entrance to village and stay outside town walls - next to bakery on corner of Calle Rusticiana and Avenida del Puente Romano. Camping Merendero by old bridge on leaving town also serves food when open. PS in *ayuntamiento*.
The town is inside a complete set of walls, now being restored to form a paseo *both along the top and round the outside, an alcázar and church of Santa María with Mudéjar apse and scallops in groups of five in decorative ironwork in north portal. Take a walk round the ramparts (several access points) to get a good view of the town and its surrounding area. Its three* puertas *are still intact: Puerta del Rey, Puerta de Santa María and Puerta de la Villa. Walkway outside the town walls as well.*

6km Aldeahuela del Jerte (378/622) Bar in *Hogar del Pensionista*, shop, farmacia.

5km Carcaboso 271m (383/617)
Bars, shops, bank (no CD), Rte "Las Golondrinas" (has key for basic R&F, no shower, reported very hot). Bar Pacense is now Bar Ruta de la Plata (on main road) and has recently modernised inexpensive rooms, reported very pilgrim-friendly. Owner will phone Hostal Asturias in Jarilla for you (for next night's accommodationh) if required (see below under Cáparra).
Modern church of Santiago Apóstol with glass roundel of Santiago Matamoros above west door.
Make sure you have enough water before you leave here as there are *no facilities at all for 35km,* till you reach the bar on the N630, 4km before Aldeanueva.
Plasencia (11km to the east, all facilities) did not exist in Roman times and so was not on the route of the Vía de la Plata, but is well worth a visit. Hotel Rincón Extremadura, Bar Micasa, Pensión Blanco and Hostal Muralla all have rooms. Its casco antiguo (historic quarter) contains the old and new cathedrals, several churches and historic houses and the town had seven pilgrim hospitals in medieval times.

Note: there are two buses a day (and back) to Plasencia from Carcaboso but both leave early in the morning, returning mid afternoon. If you want to have a rest day and visit Plasencia it is therefore easier (logistically) to spend 2 nights in Carcaboso so that you an make an early start from there when you leave to continue your journey.

13km Venta Quemada (396/604)
Isolated house at side of road. No facilities of any kind thougyh the owners are reported willing to provide pilgrims with water if needed.

The next stretch of the camino is very beautiful, quiet and peaceful, along a very wide walled lane, with a fair amount of shade and good views into the distance (the Embalse de Gabriel y Galán and a national park are over to the west).

6.5km Cáparra 400m (402.5/587.5)
Owner of Hostal Asturias in Jarilla (on N630, tel: 927.47.70.57) will collect you from the arch between 16.30 and 17.00 hrs if you phone the evening before. Alternatively you can continue from Caparra for another 5km more and then turn R and walk there (an additional 2km); in either case you can return to the *camino* the following morning by turning R out of the hostal, R again and then R once you rejoin the *camino*. This avoids what would otherwise be a *very* long stage (38kms from Carcaboso to Aldeanueva).

Remains of ancient Roman city with four-square triumphal arch, surrounded by fields. This is no mere museum piece, however, and the camino *actually passes underneath it. It has now become more "touristy," with aq visitor's centre, though this means that you can now get into the ruins of the adjacent town.*

18.5km Aldeanueva del Camino 529m (421/579)
Shops, bars. New small *refugio* (4pl. downstairs, 5 up, hot showers, no charge but leave donation), key either from 1st bar on L after bridge in centre of village ("Bar La Union") or from lady in house 2 doors from refuge towards centre. Hostal/Rte Montesol at end of village (open all year) has inexpensive rooms (tel: 927.48.43.35) and dies meals. Fountain with good (chlorine-free) drinking water (hard L in centre of village).

San Servando, one of the town's two parish churches, has modern tiled Santiago panel above high altar.

Detour (total 8km) recommended to **Hervás** *(pop. 3,500, accom. available). Apart from the Palacio de los Dávilas, the Convento Trinitario and the church of Santa María, it contains the best-preserved* judería *(Jewish quarter) in Spain. To return to the Vía de la Plata do not retrace your steps to the N630 the way you came but rejoin it further to the north by taking the SECOND turning.*

10km Baños de Montemayor 708m (431/569)
Small spa town with shops, bars, banks. *Albergue turístico* (tel: 679.22.82.08) and plenty of other accommodation (one hotel, five hostales and four fondas). Campsite "Las Cañadas" (Cat.1) at KM432 on N630. Tourist Office in the *ayuntamiento. Vía de la Plata* information centre.

A rather "touristy"'place where people still go to "take the waters" and a lot of basketwork (cestería) is on sale. Thermal baths of Roman origin (with small museum), famous for the cure of respiratory and muscular complaints. Church of Santa María (the second church is now a cultural centre).

SUMMARY OF SANTIAGO AND PILGRIM REFERENCES

(a) Seville to Astorga

Seville 1. Cathedral a) Puerta de San Miguel has carving of Santiago Peregrino b) Capilla de Santiago has painting of St James the Great at the battle of Clavijo by Juan de Roelas, 1609, on R as well as stained-glass window of Battle of Clavijo. 2. Hospital de la Caridad has statue of San Roque with scallops and staff in chapel, on RH side of main altarpiece.

Almadén de la Plata formerly had church dedicated to Santiago.

Calera de León Conventual de Santiago, monastery of Order of Santiago founded by Pelay Pérez in 1275, master of Order of Santiago a) Painting behind high altar in monastery church of Nuestra Señora de la Asunción depicts knights carrying banner of Order of Santiago in battle against Moors b) Stained glass of apse contains swords of Santiago.

Monasterio de Nuestra Señora de Tentudía Belonged to Order of Santiago. Italian tiled altarpiece in RH Santiago chapel with Santiago Matamoros.

Fuente de Cantos Church of Nuestra Señora de la Granada has statue of San Roque inside on R and statue of Santiago Apóstol (with shells on each lapel) on altar mayor.

Calzadilla de los Barros Town coat of arms contains scallop shell and sword of Santiago.

Zafra 1. Hospital de Santiago (now mental hospital), founded by los Condes de Feria in 1457. 2. Colegiata de Nuestra Señora de la Candelaria has statue of Santiago Apóstol to upper R of main altar. 3. Arco del Cubo, Campo de Rosario, has equestrian Santiago bas-relief.

Los Santos de Maimona 1. Town coat of arms with Cruz de Santiago. 2. Palacio de la Encomienda (command headquarters of military Order of Santiago) is now ayuntamiento. 3. Church of Nuestra Señora de los Angeles has a) Puerta del Perdón and b) lion with sword of Santiago above door. Town formerly belonged to Knights of Santiago and had five ermitas, including one from 1504 onwards dedicated to Santiago.

Villafranca de los Barros Church of Santa María del Valle has a) much shell decoration inside: shells on collars around pillars of south porch, south nave and around south nave portal b) statue of San Roque with very large scallop shell, staff and big leg wound in south porch c) Santiago Apóstol with book and shell in main altarpiece on RH side, centre, of main altarpiece. (Town also belonged to Knights of Santiago.)

Almendralejo Another town reconquered from Moors by Order of Santiago (1241). 1. Church of Purificación de Nuestra Señora has escutcheon incorporating scallop and sword of Santiago in apse. 2. Capilla de Santiago. 3. Church of San Roque in western suburbs.

Torremegía Palacio del Marquesado de Torremegía has ring of huge scallops around Renaissance main portal.

Mérida 1. Church of Santa María (church of last Master of ithe Order of Santiago) has escutcheon incorporating scallops and cross of Santiago on west door. 2. Church of Santa Eulalia has stone bas-relief of Santiago Peregrino with hat and staff on pulpit.

Aljucén Church of San Andrés (inside) has Santiago crosses on all its pedestals.

Casas de Don Antonio 1. Ermita de Nuestra Señora del Pilar at exit to village has two depictions of Santiago a) relief sculpture of Santiago Apóstol, with hat, on altarpiece and b) tiny statue of Santiago Matamoros on prancing horse, taken on annual romería on May 1st to: 2. Ermita de Casa de Santiago Bencaliz (which has very small Roman bridge behind it).

Cáceres 1. Town coat of arms includes sword of Santiago, scallop shells. 2. Escutcheon of sword of Santiago and scallop shells on façade of a) Palacio de Hernando de Ovando, Plaza Santa María and b) in cloister in Casa de Lorenzo de Ulloa, Calle Ancha. 3. Iglesia de Santiago a) bas-relief of pilgrim with staff, scrip, hat, shell above north portal (first pilgrim figure on journey) b) collars of scallop shells encircle north portal pillars c) Baroque main altarpiece has huge Santiago Matamoros at Clavijo d) south chapel has wooden chairs with scallop shells on back e) stained glass in apse contains sword of Santiago. 4. Iglesia de Santa María a) relief sculpture of Santiago Matamoros in main altarpiece (sixteenth century, possibly by Roque Balduque) b) wooden sculpture of Santiago Peregrino.

Casar de Cáceres 1. Iglesia de la Asunción in centre of village has Baroque wood painted Santiago on LH side of main altarpiece with fine Santiago Peregrino complete with staff, gourd, hat and scallop. Modern but inverted black scallop in grille of southwest chapel. 2. Ermita de Santiago, at end of village, has modern Santiago Matamoros with giant sword above altar.

Cañaveral Sixteenth-century Ermita de San Roque.

Galisteo Church of Santa María has scallops in groups of five in decorative ironwork in north portal.

Carcaboso Modern church of Santiago Apóstol with glass roundel of Santiago Matamoros above west door.

Plasencia 1. New Cathedral: Santiago Peregrino on main altarpiece (bottom R). 2. Old Cathedral: scallop shell decoration on pillars in its cloisters. 3. Old Cathedral museum has eighteenth-century statue of Santiago Apóstol. 4. Sculpture of Santiago Peregrino in town walls.

Aldeanueva del Camino San Servando, one of its two parish churches, has modern tiled Santiago panel above high altar.

Baños de Montemayor A casa-hospital belonging to ayuntamiento in Plaza de la Alberguería existed here until nineteenth century.

Valverde de Valdelacasa 1. Iglesia de Santiago. 2. Calle Camino de Santiago. 3. Remains of former hospital, 1704 in lintel, with Santiago cross in coat of arms.

Fuenterrobles de Salvatierra Formerly had both ermita and hospital dedicated to Santiago; latter was demolished in 1770 due to bad condition. Was also Santiago fountain in area, near Sierra de Tanda.

Pico de la Dueña now topped by sword of Santiago.

Salamanca 1. Twelfth-century brick church of Santiago by Roman bridge with sword of Santiago in escutcheon on west front. 2. Old Cathedral a) Talavera chapel: shield with scallop shells b) Salas Capitalinas: statue of Santiago Apóstol with book, dressed in white c) Santa Catalina chapel: statue of San Roque d) Anaya chapel has marble bas-relief of Santiago Peregrino on base of tomb of Don Gutiérrez de Monroy and tiny alabaster bas-relief of heavily bearded Santiago with other apostles along base of alabaster tomb of Bishop Anaya. 3. New Cathedral: painted wood statue of Santiago Apóstol in north aisle of Capilla de Santiago. 4. Convento de Sancti Spiritu, its church associated with the Order of Santiago: a) Santiago Matamoros in pediment of north portal b) Santiago Matamoros in pediment of south portal with medallion of head of Santiago Peregrino L, above south portal c) painted Santiago Matamoros in centre of main altarpiece d) stone Santiago Apóstol in north aisle. 5. Colegio Arzobispo Fonseca (Irish College): medallion of Santiago Matamoros above main portal and frieze of scallop shells. 6. Corner of Calle Cervantes and Calle Rabanal: shell escutcheon. 7. Convento de las Dueñas: medallion of San Roque and shell motifs in lower cloister. 8. University – Patio de las Escuelas: shell decoration in ironwork of main doorway. 9. Casa de las Conchas, civilian residence so named for its shell-covered facade, built c. 1490 by Dr Rodrigo Arias Talavera Maldonado, knight of the Order of the Knights of Santiago in Salamanca. 10. Museum has statue with attributes of Santiago Apóstol with shell on hat.

Calzada de Valdunciel Statue of Santiago Peregrino in church of Santa Elena, in sandals and with no hat.

Villanueva de Campeán Calle de Santiago.

Zamora 1. Twelfth-century Romanesque church of Santiago del Burgo has painted bas-relief of Santiago Matamoros above painted wooden statue of Santiago Apóstol with staff and book on main altarpiece. 2. Second Santiago church, outside town walls, tiny Romanesque Ermita de Santiago de los Caballeros. 3. Church of San Claudio de Olivares has statue of San Roque Peregrino. 4. Cathedral: gilded statue of Santiago Peregrino with hat, scallop, gourd and staff in niche on RH side of chancel. 5. Cathedral museum: painting of head of Santiago on RH side of predella of wall-mounted San Ildefonso altarpiece.

Castrotorafe Ruins of Castillo, seat of Order of the Knights of Santiago.

Benavente Former Hospital de la Piedad has pilgrim doorknocker and scallops incorporated into arms of founder on main facade. Modern church of Santiago in suburbs.

Alija del Infantado Modern Cruz del Orden de Santiago on hill high to R above village at exit.

La Bañeza Hospital donated to church of El Salvador in 932 for pilgrims and other needy.

Astorga contained twenty-two pilgrim hospitals in the Middle Ages, the last of which, the Hospital de las Cinco Llagas (the Five Wounds), burned down early in the 20th century. 1. Cathedral: i) tiny statue of *Santiago Peregrino* above main west portal; ii) bas-relief of procession of pilgrims, tympanum of west portal;   iii) statue of Santiago, chapel of north wall;   iv) painting of Santiago among other apostles on the side of a wooden chest from the Cistercian monastery of Carrizo de la Ribera, in the diocesan museum. 2. Museo de los Caminos, Palacio Episcopal has several stone/polychrome/wood statues of Santiago. 3. Church of San Pedro, main facade covered in pilgrim themes: mosaics - route, churches, hospitals and pilgrims - prepared for *Las Edades de del Hombre* (exhibition) in 2000.

(b) Tábara to Santiago

Santa Marta de Tera Santiago Peregrino statue in LH portal of south door.

Pumarejo de Tera Church dedicated to Santiago.

Olleros de Tera Formerly had pilgrim hospital.

Rionegro del Puente 1. Former pilgrim hospital (building still exists). 2. Former church of Santiago (only tower left) is now cemetery chapel. 3. Cofradía de los Falifos, oldest such organisation devoted to looking after pilgrims, still functioning. 4. Santuario de Nuestra Señora de Carballada has freestanding statues of St. James as pilgrim on RH side wall inside and St. Roch as pilgrim (on left).

Triufé House that was formerly pilgrim hospital still standing.

Terroso Church dedicated to Santiago.

Campobecerros Church dedicated to Santiago with modern statue of Santiago pilgrim/apostle in niche over front door and representation of Santiago Matamoros inside building.

Laza Church contains depictions of Virgen del Rosario, Santiago and San Roque Peregrino on main altarpiece.

Albergueria Site of former pilgrim hospital. Statue of Santiago inside church of Santa María.

Vilar de Barrio Scallop shell in town coat of arms.

Xunqueira de Ambía 'Virgen Peregrina' in Baroque pilgrim outfit on side altar of twelfth-century church. St. James pilgrim on LH side altar, St. Roch pilgrim on RH side altar..

Ourense 1. Cathedral a) Pórtico del Paraíso has seated statue of Santiago, against pillar; sword in RH, open book in LH, with text facing viewer, no hat, three scallop shells at base of column. b) Statue of Santiago Matamoros in interior over north door. c) 16th c. polychrome Santiago Peregrino set in grille. d) Tiny stone bas-relief of Santiago Peregrino above north portal (part of Deposition scene). 2. Claustro de San Francisco has statue of Santiago Peregrino with scrip, scallop, tau and book on north-east pillar in cloister. 3. Tiny statue of Santiago Peregrino (stone, modern) above a Romanesque tympanum built into moden building on LH side of Avenida de Zamora (on way into town).

Albarellos de Monterrei Church with statue of Santiago Peregrino on south wall.

Monterrey Ruins of eighteenth-century pilgrim hospital in hilltop castle complex.

Xinzo de Limia Romanesque church of Santa Mariña has a) freestanding statue of San Roque on LH side of chancel arch b) capital of a face above giant scallop to RH side of west portal.

Piñeira de Arcos Modern cruceiro with statue of Santiago Peregrino on shaft.

Allariz Church dedicated to Santiago. Both this and church of San Estevo have statues of San Roque Peregrino inside.

Faramontaos Village formerly had pilgrim hospital.

Oseira Formerly had pilgrim hospital. a) Monastery church of Santa María la Real has Baroque altarpiece with painting of Santiago Peregrino. b) Monastery cloister has polychrome statue of Santiago Peregrino in niche in north-east corner of upper Galeria de Claustro Procesional.

Puxallos Ermita de San Roque.

Taboada Church of Santiago has a) painting of Santiago Matamoros in Baroque altarpiece inside building b) modern statue of Santiago Peregrino in sitting area outside.

Bandeira Formerly had pilgrim hospital.

Capilla de Santiaguiño (between Ponte Ulla and Susana) 1. Chapel dedicated to Santiago, built 1696, restored 2000. 2. Fountain with statue of Santiago Peregrino in niche above it.

Santiago de Compostela 1. Cathedral: i) statue of St. James and his companions Anastasius and Theodore above the Puerta Santa; ii) Platerías facade - spindly Santiago Apóstol is to Christ's R in the Apostles frieze above the portal; iii) Azabachería facade - *Santiago Peregrino* flanked by kneeling figures of Alfonso VI and Ordono II at the very top of the facade above the doors; iv) Obradoiro facade: a) centre top *Santiago Peregrino;* b) above entrance to crypt - tiny bas-relief of *Santiago Matamoros.;* v) Pórtico de la Gloria: a) St. James seated with tau cross on the trumeau and scroll; b) *Santiago Apóstol,* right panel of Apostles; vi) *Santiago Matamoros:* a) west side of north Azabachería arm of the transept - statue in glass case; b) Clavijo tympanum - stone bas-relief of *Santiago Matamoros,* west side of the south, Platerías arm of the transept; vii) Polychrome statue of *Santiago Peregrino,* altarpiece of Capilla de San Bartolomé, northeast ambulatory; viii) Capilla de las Reliquias, south aisle has: a) Gilded statuette of Santiago Coquatriz; b) gilded statue of *Santiago Peregrino* of Don Alvaro de Isorno; c) *Santiago Peregrino* - tiny silver statue; ix) Niche statue of *Santiago Peregrino,* west wall of the south (Platerías) arm of the transept above the door to the Sacristy; x) Stained glass seated *Santiago Peregrino* in the ambulatory above the Holy Door (the inside one); xi) Chancel - Capilla Mayor has: a) *Santiago Matamoros* crowning the baldechín; b) *Santiago Peregrino* standing on top of the Camerín; c) Seated *Santiago Peregrino* in the camarín - the "hug" Santiago; xii) Neo-Romanesque silver casket containing the body of St. James and his disciples Anastasius and Theodore in the crypt under the Capilla Mayor; xiii) Cloister: *Santiago Peregrino,* left side of the altarpiece of the Transfiguration of Christ,

Capilla de Alba, NW corner of cloister;   xiv) Polychrome statue of *Santiago Peregrino*, left side of altarpiece of Capilla del Salvador (chapel of the Kings of France), axial chapel of ambulatory.   xv) Museum of the Cathedral: a) seated stone polychrome Santiago with tau cross and crown; b) bronze relief of the Translation of the body of the Apostle to Galicia; c) polychrome wood and alabaster retablo of the Life of St. James, donated by John Goodyear - the Calling, Martyrdom and Translation; d) gilded wood panel of Queen Lupa's stubborn oxen and the apostle's body in the cart in Galicia; e) gilded wood reredos of pilgrims climbing the hill to Santiago; f) gilded wood panel of Moors returning the bells from Córdoba to Santiago; g) polychrome wood relief of Santiago preaching in Galicia.

2. Colegio de San Geronimo - north portal, statue of *Santiago Peregrino*, left side.

3. Palacio de Rajoy: *Santiago Matamoros* crowning a triangular pediment of bas-relief of *Santiago Matamoros* at the Battle of Clavijo - main facade.

4. Hostal de los Reyes Católicos: i) statue of *Santiago Peregrino*, top left upper frieze above the main south portal; ii) statue of *Santiago Peregrino* - centre of the lower frieze of the Apostles above the main south portal; iii) statue of St. James, right jamb of main south portal.

5. Monasterio de San Martín Pinario (in its museum): i) statue of the Virgen del Pilar and Child appearing to a kneeling *Santiago Apóstol;* ii) statue of *Santiago Matamoros.*

6. Colegiata de Santa María del Sar: i) statue of *San Roque Peregrino* in vestry; ii) statue of *San Roque Peregrino* in north apse.

7. Pilgrimage museum: *i)* Wood relief, *San Roque Peregrino* ii) Wood statue of a pilgrim iii) Polychrome wood panel painting of Christ as a pilgrim iv) Polychrome wood statue, *San Roque Peregrino*, back of a chest v) Santa Isabel, "Reina de Portugal Aragonesa" - dressed as a lady pilgrim   vi) Polychrome *Santiago Peregrino* - 8 wood ones. vii) Polychrome granite *Santiago Peregrino* viii) Polychrome wood 'Virgen Peregrina' with child ix) Stone statue *Santiago Peregrino* 3 stone ones x) Tapestry/embroidery of *Santiago Apóstol.*

8. Statue of St. James above a fountain near Santo Domingo de Bonneval

9. Colegio de Santiago Alfeo/de Fonseca - statue of *Santiago Peregrino* above main portal

10. Huge modern statue of *Santiago Peregrino* in middle of roundabout outside the Xunta de Galica headquarters in the San Caetano area of Santiago (near bus station).

NOTES

NOTES

BAÑOS de MONTEMAYOR – SALAMANCA

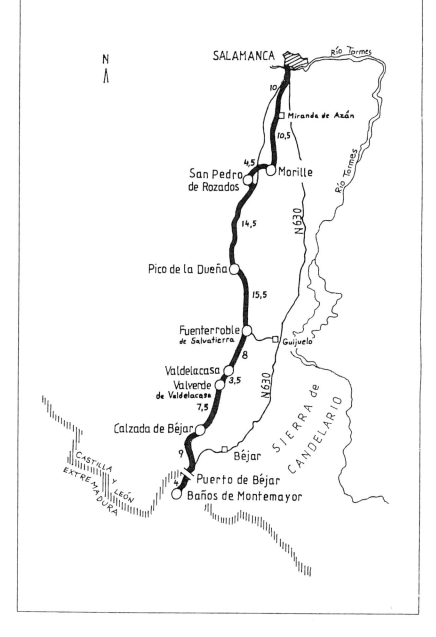

N

SALAMANCA

Río Tormes

10

Miranda de Azán

10,5

Río Tormes

4,5

San Pedro de Rozados Morille

N630

14,5

Pico de la Dueña

15,5

Fuenterroble de Salvatierra Guijuelo

8

Valdelacasa

3,5

Valverde de Valdelacasa

N630

7,5

Calzada de Béjar

SIERRA de CANDELARIO

9

Béjar

CASTILLA Y LEÓN

EXTREMADURA

4

Puerto de Béjar

Baños de Montemayor

3.5km Puerto de Béjar 870m (434.5/565/5)

Bar/rte on L. *Refugio* in old school, 300m past the petrol station (with café). Casa Adriano has PS and does meals. *Casa Rural?* Info. welcome.

4km Puente de la Magdalena (Malena) 650m (438.5/561/5)

Many miliarios *nearby in this section.*

5.5km Calzada de Béjar 796m (444/556)

Bar, fountain, R&F in *Casa Consistorial* (ask in bar, which does simple meals). New private refugio "Alba Soroya" directly on *camino* at entrance to town (tel: 923.41.65.05 or 646.41.06.43, good reports), 10 beds, meals if required. *Casa Rural* (ask in bar, also has kitchen).
Church of Nuestra Señora de la Asunción.

9km Valverde de Valdelacasa (453/547)

Fountain, bar at end of village in *Hogar del Pensionista* (unmarked, in former school, not always open).
Church of Santiago. Former pilgrim hospital in house with 1704 over the door and Santiago sword in coat of arms.

3.5km Valdelacasa 964m (456.5/543.5)

Two bars, shop behind church. *Centro de día* does meals.
Originally there was only one house here – hence the village's name.

Cyclists may wish to make a 10km detour here to **Guijelo** for accommodation (shops, banks, Hotel Torres – tel: 923.58.14.51, Pensión Comercial). If so you can return to the *camino* the following day by taking the minor road to Fuenterroble de Salvatierra: from the N630 cross the railway line, turn R and follow its windings for 6km to Fuenterroble.

7.5km Fuenterroble de Salvatierra 955m (464/536)

Shop in "Bar Ultramarinos", meals in second bar ("El pesebre"). *Refugio* (and PS) in *Casa Parroquial*, run by Don Blas Rodríguez, the very helpful parish priest; the ashes of the late José Luis Salvador Salvador, former president of the Seville 'Amigos', are buried in the front wall of the building.
Fortress church of Santa María la Blanca,impressively restored and now in use again as the parish church, after being closed for decades. Enormous modern statue (in wood) of Christ risen from the dead inside, taken on a pilgrimage around nearby villages before being placed in situ. (Useful information board near church and parque temático showing the construction of Roman roads and explaining Roman burial customs, miliarios, and the Vía de la Plata.) Ermita del Santo Cristo.

15.5km Pico de la Dueña 1140m (479.5/520.5)

Highest point on the route with spectacular views on a clear day. The "pico" itself is now surmounted by a modern cross of the Order of Santiago and forms a sort of "Cruz de Ferro" for the Vía de la Plata.
The number of wayside crosses you pass on the way up varies from year to year as a new one is added every Good Friday, part of a chain that will form a Vía Crucis (Stations of

the Cross) when it is finished. The cross atop the Pico *itself will then form #14, the last one in the series.*

5.5km Calzadilla de Mendigos 950m (485/515)

A large pig farm on the road (it has its name on it). *For pilgrims going all the way to Santiago from Seville this is roughly the halfway point on their journey.* Pilgrims who have run out off water report that owners will fill your water bottle for you.

8km San Pedro de Rozados (980m) (493/507)

Two bars, *panadería*, shop but no fountain. Ask in Bar Moreno for R&F in old school; the bar's owner, Maricarmen, also does hot meals on request and has a pilgrim stamp and book. New *Casa Rural* planned: info.welcome.

4.5km Morille (497.5/502.5) Fountain, bar (opens late). New small refugio (5 beds) in *Centro Médico*, good reports (keys with María José, tel: 923.34.40.18).

10.5km Miranda de Azán (508/492) 2 bars, shop.

10km Salamanca 808m, pop. 167,000 (530/461)

All facilities, RENFE, buses to Madrid, Zamora, León and other parts of Spain. New municpal refugio, "Casa de la Calera," next to the *Huerto de Calixto y Melibea* (a public garden), 100m from the cathedral. (After crossing the *Puente Romano* turn R along the *Paseo del Rector Esperabe*.)

Other accommodation in all price brackets, including Hostal Peña de Francia (Calle de San Pablo 96, tel: 923.21.66.87), Fonda Barez (Calle Melendez, tel: 923.21.74.95), Pensión Estefania (Calle Jesús 3–5) and Pensión Romero (Plaza Mayor) . Note, however, that it is *extremely difficult* to find accommodation in Salamanca at weekends, in the summer and on publoic holidays.

Campsite 2.5km out of town towards Zamora. CRS: Bicicletas Palacios, Avenida de los Reyes de España 6, Bicicletas Gilfer, Calle Bólivar 43 and La Cadena, Calle Vitigudin 17. PS is available from the kiosk in the cathedral and also from the office of the church of San Marcos, 12.30 to 13.30hrs, on *camino* out of town.

Another place to spend a whole day. Tourist Office: Gran Vía 11 and a second office in arch in Plaza Mayor (ask for leaflet with walking tour of city). Two cathedrals (Old and New), university (founded by Alfonso IX in 1218), Plaza Mayor, Patio de las Escuelas, Casa de las Conchas, and many churches and convents, including church of San Tomás de Canterbury. Capilla de Santiago (12th c. Romanesque-Mudéjar style) outside historic quarter, by river. Museum in Old Cathedral (fee) has statue of St James.

Useful bar open 6.00hrs, corner of Avda de Portugal (on *camino* just past Iglesia San Marcos).

6.5km Aldeaseca de la Armuña 820m (524.5/475.5)

Bars, rte by petrol station, shop, farmacia, bank (+CD), fountain in public garden.

5km Castellanos de Villiquera 830m (529.5/470.5)

Two bars, shop, farmacia.

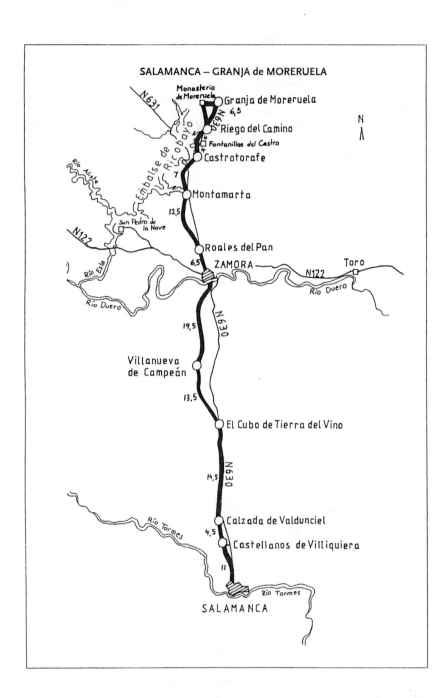

SALAMANCA – GRANJA de MORERUELA

Monasterio de Moreruela
N631
Granja de Moreruela
N630
6,5
Riego del Camino
Fontanillos del Castro
Castrotorafe
7
Embalse de Ricobayo
Río Aliste
Montamarta
12,5
San Pedro de la Nave
N122
Roales del Pan
6,5
ZAMORA
N122
Toro
Río Esla
Río Duero
Río Duero
19,5
N630
Villanueva de Campeán
13,5
El Cubo de Tierra del Vino
14,5
N630
Río Tormes
Calzada de Valdunciel
4,5
Castellanos de Villiquiera
11
Río Tormes
SALAMANCA

N

4.5km Calzada de Valdunciel 807m (534/466)
2 bars (but no food), shop, bank, fountain in square. New municipal *refugio* (8 beds, hot showers, kitchen, leave donation) - key from Elena in house behind *Casa Consistorial.* Hostal/Rte El Pozo 500m to east on N630 (tel: 923.31.00.16) has rooms and is nearest place for meals.
Church of Santa Elena contains altar with Santiago Peregrino.

20km El Cubo de Tierra del Vino 846m (554/446)
Bar Santo Domingo (on L, entering village) does meals and has rooms (mixed reports), 2 other bars (no food), shop, farmacia.
Refugio in church, ask priest (Don Tomás), 3€ donation expected. R&F: does the *Alcasdesa* (mayoress) in house opp. school still offer this faility? Info.welcome. Rooms also reported available in Calle Garcia la Serna 13 (Señora Carmen).
The village takes its name from the fact that this area, south of the Río Duero, is rich in vines, whereas the region to its north, the Tierra del Pan, is mainly cornfields. You are now in the province of Zamora.
Note first of a series of decorative terracotta plaques in main street, indicating position of the village on the Vía de la Plata. These have been placed in all towns and villages along the route in the province of Zamora by the Fundación Ramos de Castro, frequently on or near the cchurch. They are all in the same general style but each one provides information and references specific to its situation and local history.

13km Villanueva de Campeán 765m (567/433)
Fountain in main square, shop. Bar Jambarina (Calle del Señor 12) is now closed due to owner's ill-health but a new bar (with food) now open. Very small municipal *refugio* with bunks and hot shower.
Two waymarked routes after Villanueva: one by-passes village of San Marcial *(bar)*, the other (easier for cyclists) that leads directly to it.

19km Zamora 658m, pop. 64,421 (586/414)
All facilities, RENFE, buses to León, Ourense, Madrid and other parts of Spain. Plenty of accommodation: 10 hotels, 11 hostales and 10 pensiones, including Rte/Pensión La Alistan (Calle Libertad, near Tres Cruces), Bar Jarame (outside city walls), Bar El Jardín (near church of San Torcuato), Fonda Padornelo and Hostal la Reina (Plaza Mayor). No *refugio* at present but one reported in preparation in building adjoining the church of San Ciprano: info. welcome. *Sello: Policía local* or parish churches (such as San Ildefonso). CRS: La Madrileña, Calle San Andrés 19.
NB: There are **no cash dispensers** before Benavente if you are going to Santiago via Astorga.
Town situated on north bank of Río Duero, developed and expanded by the Romans on the site of an existing centre of population. Cathedral and 19 Romanesque churches: Santiago del Burgo (Santiagos Matamoros and Peregrino on main altar reredos), San Juan de Puerta Nueva, Santa María la Nueva, San Cipriano, San Ildefonso, La Magdalena, Santa María de la Horta and Santo Tomé, as well as the cathedral, are all open to the public daily except Mondays, from 10.00 to 13.00 hrs and 17.00 to 20.00 hrs. San Claudio de Olivares (contains statue of San Roque as a pilgrim) and Santiago de los Caballeros, both on the western outskirts, are open the same hours but July–September only. Other chuirches are open at mas times whereas San Estéban is now the Museo Baltasar Lobo,

exhibiting the sculptures and drawings of the internationally renowned Zamoran artist who died in 1993.

Zamora is also well known for its week-long Semana Santa (Holy Week) processions (accommodation very difficult during this period) and many of the floats used, both modern and historic, are in the Museo de la Semana Santa (others are located in different churches). Castillo, ramparts, Palacio Episcopal, Parador de Turismo in former palace of the Condes de Alba, Hospital de la Incarnación (now headquarters of regional government). Tourist Office, Calle de Santa Clara 20 (tel: 980.52.69.53) does guided walking tours of the town (in Spanish) every morning in summer except Mondays. Worth spending a whole day here.

6.5km Roales de Pan 700m (592.5/407.5)

Farmacia, bar, rte on N630. Refugio reported in prreparation in 2004: info.welcome.

NB: As there is often nowhere else to paint arrows in this area watch out for them on the concrete slabs that end the drain pipes of the irrigation system at junctions on the camino.

12.5km Montamarta 690m (605/395)

Bar/Rte El Asturiano (tel: 980.55.01.82) at KM262 on main road (opposite the petrol station, before you enter the village) has inexpensive rooms and meals (reported very friendly). Bars, shop and farmacia in centre, near church, and others on main road.

10km Castrotorafe (615/385)

Remains of a town, possibly dating from Roman times, and inhabited until the 18th century, controlling the traffic crossing the river Esla. Its castillo was the seat of the Knights of the Order of Santiago and is all that remains today, as the rest of the town is normally submerged in the reservoir.

2km Fontanillas de Castro 725m (617/383)

Bar/rte by petrol station 1km before village, fountain.

4km Riego del Camino 705m (621/379)

Bar on main road (with simple food), shop. R&F in attic above social club, 10 bunks, shower & toilet downstairs; key at house with green door.

6km Granja de Moreruela 708m (627/373)

Three bars on main road Bar Peregrino,up the hill on the turn-off to the Astorga route, does (copious) meals, is open early for bkft, has *sello* and pilgrim book and is very pilgrim-friendly (ring bell if it appears closed). It also has the key to the refugio; the facilties in the Casa de la Cultura (on the main road at entry to village) were being renovated and upgraded (bunks, new plumbing) during 2004 (during which accommodation was temporarily available in a house opposite) but should now be ready. Shop.

This is where the two caminos divide, one continuing ahead (north) to Astorga, the other turning left (west) to go directly to Santiago via Puebla de Sanabria and Ourense. To take this 2nd option turn to page 43.

*From here a detour to the west is suggested to visit the ruins of the **Convento de Moreruela**, the first Cistercian convent in Spain, founded in 1158, with a pilgrim hospital* *added in the 16th century. To do so turn L off N630 (signposted) just before entry to village, which takes you directly there, 3.7km each way. The convent is on private land and is being restored at the time of writing but it Is usually accessible and worth the detour.*

4km further on, at KM237/238 on main road, 400m after the road turning to Tábara, the Hostal Oviedo (980.56.90.45 or 980.58.60.80) has rooms and does meals but bar not open early.

* * * * * * *

Convnto de la Moreruela

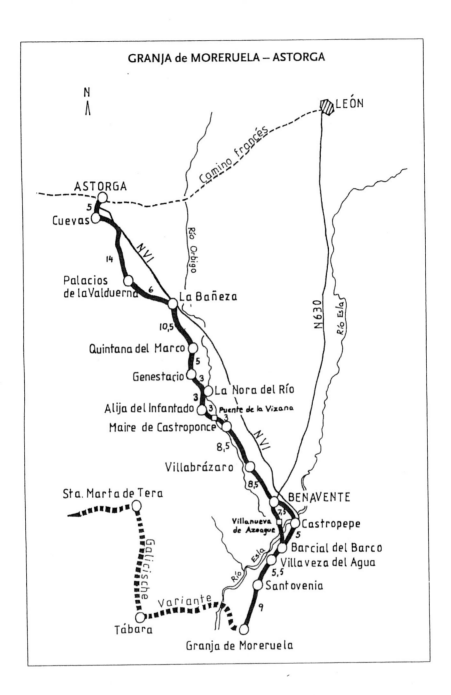

GRANJA de MORERUELA – ASTORGA

N

LEÓN

Camino francés

ASTORGA

5

Cuevas

14

NVI

Río Orbigo

Palacios
de la Valduerna

6

La Bañeza

10,5

N630

Río Esla

Quintana del Marco

5

Genestacio

3

La Nora del Río

3

Alija del Infantado

3

Puente de la Vizana

Maire de Castroponce

3

8,5

NVI

Villabrázaro

8,5

Sta. Marta de Tera

BENAVENTE

7,5

Villanueva
de Azoague

Castropepe

Galicische

5

Barcial del Barco

Río Esla

Villaveza del Agua

5,5

Santovenia

Variante

9

Tábara

Granja de Moreruela

ROUTE TO ASTORGA

8.5km Santovenia 715m (635)
Bar/Rte Esla (tel: 980.64.70.14) has rooms, another bar, two shops. Fountain at end of village on R.

The "Santovenia" of the village's name refers to Santa Eugenia la Mozárabe (see plaque on church about her).

6km Villaveza del Agua 700m (641)
Bar (still with rte?) at end of village on L.

2.5km Barcial del Barco 717m (643.5)
Three bars.

6km Villanueva del Azoague 9649.5)
Bar in Plaza Mayor.

3km Benavente 747m, pop. 12,500 (652.5)
All facilities. Refugio in the old RENFE station building (key from Policia Local or Tourist office). Other accommodation in all price brackets (three hotels, eight hostales, five pensiones), including Fonda California (Primo de Rivera 32, tel: 980.63.38.34), Hostal Ría de Vigo (Primo de Rivera 27, tel: 980.63.17.79) and Hostal Paraíso (Calle Obispo Regueras 64, tel: 980.63.33.81). *Sello: ayuntamiento*, between 8.00 and 15.00 hrs. Tourist Office in Calle Fortaleza 17.

Old town has churches of Santa María del Azoque and San Juan del Mercado (both open for visits 10.00 to 13.00 and 517.00 to 20.00 hrs), Hospital de la Piedad (former pilgrim hospice with cloister and pilgrim door knocker in early 16th c.entrance) and Ermita de la Soledad. Castillo de la Mota is now the parador(only tower - the Torre de Caracol - remains of original building). Modern octagonal church of Santiago in northern suburbs.

8km Villabrázaro 710m (660.5)
Large bar at entrance to village (has pilgrim book and does simple food), unmarked shop in main street (RH side), fountain in centre of village. Simple *refugio* for those with pilgrim *credencial*. *Sello* in the *ayuntamiento*.

Plaque informs you that the village was a mansio on the Vía de la Plata in Roman times.

8.5km Maire de Castroponce 748m (669) Bar inside *Casa Consistorial*.

3km Puente de la Vizana (672)
Hostal Puente La Vizana has rooms and bar/rte (tel: 987.69.20.63, closed Thur. eve.?).

Original bridge of Roman origin but with later additions and alterations. Boundary of provinces of Zamora and León. Picnic area with trees, campsite.

From here to La Bañeza the landscape becomes much greener, though there is not necessarily more shade to walk in.

3km Alija del Infantado 740m (675)
Bars, shop, farmacia, bank (+CD), small *refugio* (6 bunks, shower, in Calle Genestacio above Bar de los Jubilados – ask in tourist office (which also has *sello*); key from Señora

Maruca, Calle Alta 7 (near church of San Estéban).

Iglesia San Estéban (13th-14th c.), Iglesia de San Verísimo (12th-16th c.), Castillo-Palacio (1st-6th c.), Fuente de Mendaña. Fuente de San Ignacio of Roman origin, with water with medicinal properties (digestion, obesity, kidney problems), Rincón de la Judería (former Jewish quarter) with a lot of bodegas (on top of hill near fountain). Small ermita on LH side of road at entrance to village by children's playground was formerly in private hands but is now owned by a fundación that is constructing leisure and sports facilities there for the village. Ermita del Cristo at end of village on R and on hill at end, above it, Cruz de Peregrino (with Santiago sword).

From here to La Bañeza there are now *three* routes. One goes along minor roads via the villages of **Genestacio** (4km, bar), **Quintana del Marco** (2km but not near road), **Villanueva de Jamuz** (3km, bar in *Hogar del Pensionista*) and **Santa Elena de Jamuz** (4km). The second follows the river Jamuz for much of the way (its RH bank - turn L immediately after crossing the road bridge at the entry to **La Nora del Río**, 3km from Alija); this skirts **Quintana del Marco** (6km, bar), **Villanueva de Jamuz** (3km) and rejoins the road route at the end **of Santa Elena de Jamuz** (4.5km). The third option (turn L in **La Nora del Río** itself - unmarked bar in centre) goes via **Navianos de la Vega** (2 bars) and **San Juan de Torres.**

15km La Bañeza 777m, pop. 8,501 (697)
All facilities. Buses to Madrid, Santiago, León, Seville and other parts of Spain. Large *refugio* with kitchen in converted school (corner of Calles San Roque and Bello Horizonte), key from house no. 20 opposite.

Hostal/Rte Astur (Calle Astorga 9, tel: 987.64.04.15),
Hostal Madrid (Calle Angel Riesco 3, tel: 987.64.00.21),
Hostal Roma (Calle Astorga 56, tel: 987.64.05.89),
Pensión Astelena (Calle Lepanto 4, tel: 987.64.11.13),
Fonda Industrial (Calle Ramón y Cajal 12, tel: 987.64.10.42),
Fonda El Nistal (Calle El Salvador 15, tel: 987.64.00.69),
Pensión Bar Johnny (Calle la Fuente 18, tel: 987.64.07.26); otherwise accommodation is on the outskirts of the town on the NVI.

Tourist Office: Calle Padre Miguelez s/n. CRS: González de la Torre, Calle Antonio Bordas 16. PS from church of El Salvador.

Iglesia de Santa María, Iglesia de San Salvador (both are parish churches), Capilla de Jesús Nazareno, Capilla de las Angustias. The church of El Salvador, of Romanesque origin, is on the site of one of the earliest pilgrim hospitals, founded in AD 932 (barely 100 years after the discovery of the tomb of St James in the location that was to become Santiago de Compostela).

6km Palacios de la Valduerna (703)
Bar (unmarked) on main street on L near public garden, shop, farmacia.
Tower over to L is remains of 14th c. fortress.

12km Puente Valimbre (715)
Four-arch bridge of Roman origin over Río Turienzo. Restored on several occasions, most recently in 1998.
Cyclists stay on N630 from here to Astorga.

3km Celada de la Vega (718)

Bar/mesón at junction, Hostal La Paz (tel: 987.61.52.77, rooms)

f4km Astorga 899m, pop. 14,000 (722)

All facilities, RENFE, buses to Madrid, Santiago, Seville, León, Ponferrada, Villafranca del Bierzo and other parts of Spain. Tourist Office near cathedral. Large municipal *refugio* in centre of town, large private refugio (San Javier) in street near cathedral, kitchen. Plenty of other accommodation.

A town dating from Roman times, with extensive remains of its original walls (and drains!). Astorga was (and still is) the junction of two pilgrim routes, the Camino Francés and the Camino Mozárabe or Vía de la Plata. This explains the unusually large number of pilgrim hospitals formerly in existence (there were 22 in the Middle Ages), the last of which, the Hospital de las Cinco Llagas (the Five Wounds), burned down early in the 20th century. Gothic cathedral with interesting choir stalls and museum, Bishop's Palace built by the Catalan architect Antonio Gaudí, with pilgrim museum on ground floor and chapel upstairs. Several other interesting churches, Baroque town hall. It is worth spending half a day here.

From Astorga those who wish to continue to Santiago now "turn left" along the *Camino Francés* for another 250km and in many ways this part will seem much easier. There is an extensive network of *refugios*, getting your pilgrim passport stamped is much simpler and you will also meet a lot of other pilgrims, though, as indicated in the Introduction, many people experience something of a shock when they leave the relative solitude of the *Vía de la Plata* to be plunged into the busy hustle and bustle of this much more frequented route. There are also a lot more fountains and bars on the *Camino Francés* and once you enter Galicia the weather is usually considerably cooler as well.

The continuation from Astorga to Santiago is described in the Confraternity's guide to the *Camino francés*.

* * * * * * *

Monasterio de Oseira

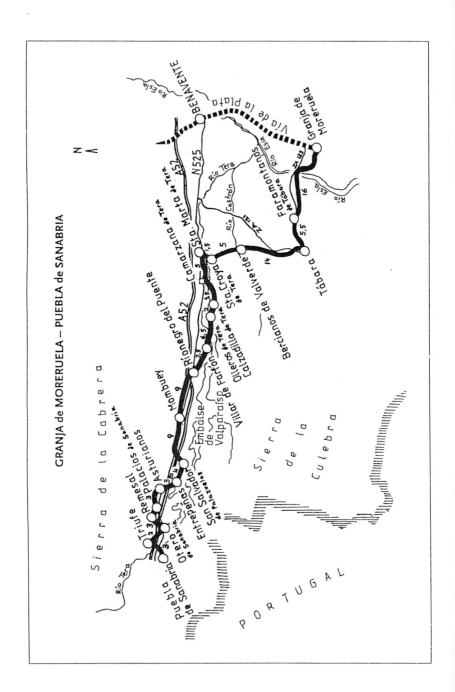

GRANJA de MORERUELA – PUEBLA de SANABRIA

ROUTE VIA PUEBLA DE SANABRIA AND OURENSE
(Camino sanabrés)

Granja de Moreruela 708m (627/373) The shorter, alternative oute from here to Puente Quintos is now fully waymarked - go uphill past Bar Peregrino, rather than taking the turning marked "Ourense" after the church.

7km Puente Quintos (634/366)
The original route crossed the Río Esla some 500m downstream, as you can see from the remains of the old bridge, positioned where you will turn away from the river after your detour to cross the present bridge.

> *Cyclists*: this section is NOT suitable, even for mountain bikes, and you should continue along the road from here to Faramontanos de Tábara.

5.5km Finca Val de la Rosa (639.5/360.5)

8km Faramontanos de Tábara (647.5/352.5)
Two bars (one with shop), another shop, panadería, no accommodation. Church porch good place for a rest.

7.5km Tábara (655/345)
Bars, shops, bank (+CD). Good refuge reported (with kitchen) - ask in *ayuntamiento* or *tabacos* on main road. Hostal Galicia (500m out of town by petrol station on road to Zamora, tel: 980.59.01.36) has rooms and rte. (To go there directly turn L along the *camino de tierra* when it bends sharp L just before some electricity pylons - instead of going straight ahead - and turn R at junction 500m later to reach main road.) PS from *tabacos* by road.
    Site of a famous monastery in Visigothic and Mozarabic periods though only a few remains and the tower are left. Two churches – 11th-century Romanesque Iglesia de la Asunción and parish church.

14km Bercianos de Valverde (669/331)
Unmarked bar (shop now closed).

7km Santa Croya de Tera (676/324) Bar, two shops, bank (no CD), farmacia,
fountain. Nice green and shady public garden is also a good place for a rest. *Casa Rural* and private refuge (Casa Anita), Calle Santa Marta 3, just before you cross bridge over river Tera into Santa Marta (tel: 980.64.52.44), good reports.

2km Santa Marta de Tera (678/322)
Two bars, shop, *refugio* accommodation in large clean room near church with mattresses and two hot showers. *Sello* from priest, who lives in modern house by church.
    12th c. Romanesque church with famous 11th c. Santiago statue in south portal. Church open for visits Fridays, Saturdays and Sundays 10.00 to 13.00 hrs, 17.00 to 20.00 hrs in winter and daily except Mondays in summer. Also open at mass times (e.g. 20.00 hrs); building next to church is former summer palace of Bishops of Astorga.
    No other accommodation in village itself but Hotel Juan Manuel (17e single, open

24/24) and Pensión Amanacer both further on (west) on main road in *Camarazana de Tera,* slightly off route, but turn L the following morning to rejoin *camino.*

6km La Barca (684/316)
Camping/recreation area with good swimming. Bar (summer only).

5km Calzadilla de Tera (689/311)
Camino does not take you through centre of village so turn L for bar, shop and panadería. (If shop is closed during posted opening hours, ring the bell.) New refugio reported in former church (donation).
   Parish church, ermita and abandoned church of Santa Justa y Rufina (is this where the new refuge is? Info.welcome).

2km Olleros de Tera (691/309)
Two bars, shop (unmarked) in Calle Fuente (near church).

8km Villar de Farfón (697/303)
Church of San Pedro (porch is a good place for a rest), fountain at end of village. No other facilities at all.

6.5km Ríonegro del Puente (703.5/296.5)
Bars, shop on main street (with *sello*), panadería on main road. Swimming area by bridge. Ask in Bar Palacios re. rooms (mixed reports).
   Former parish church of Santiago existed until the early part of the 20th century. Now only the tower remains (check for statue of St James in portal) and the present cemetery is on the site where the main body of the church used to be. Former hospital for pilgrims and travellers in building on RH side of main road, reported being renovated as a refugio in 2004 - info. welcome. Santuario de Nuestra Señora de Carballada, 15th–18th century, on the site of the original Romanesque ermita (traces in old sacristy); it belongs to the Cofradia de los Falifos (dedicated to looking after pilgrims and based in Ríonegro del Puente), one of the oldest such organisations still in existence. Free-standing statue of St. James as pilgrim (hat with scallop shell, stick, calabash and book) on RH wall of church (inside) and free-standing statue of St. Roch, also as pilgrim (hat with scallop, cape with scallop, stick, calabash, dog at his feet) on LH side wall. (Mass every evening, festival third Sunday in September.) The Palacio de Diego de Losada (diagonally across from the ayuntamiento) was restored in 1992 and is now a community centre.
   Note that from Rionegro del Puente to Mombuey there is no shade at all.

8.5km Mombuey (712/288)
All facilities. Hostal La Ruta (tel; 980.64.27.30) at KM 357 on main road, 1km before town. HR Rapina (tel: 980.65.21.20) on main road in centre (closed Sundays?); ask there for R&F in clean, small building in side street with 2 beds, 3 mattresses and hot shower.
   Romanesque parish church of Nuestra Señora de la Asunción (restored in 1992) with 13th-century tower is a National Monument, its military-type construction attributed to the Templars.
   After Mombuey the landscape begins to change and you enter, in spirit if not in fact, into Galicia.

5km Valdemerilla (717/283)
Church of San Lorenzo, fountain, but no other facilities.

3.5km Cernadilla (720.579.5) Fountain.

2km San Salvador de Palazuelos (722.5/277.5) Fountain.

3.5km Entrepeñas (726/274)
Embalse de Cernadilla 300–400m away to south.

3km Asturianos (729/271)
Three shops, mesón (food), farmacia, fountain.

3km Palacios de Sanabria (732/268)
Two bars (one with rte), shop, bank (no CD).

3km Remesal (735/265) No facilities (but plenty of dogs!).

3.5km Otero de Sanabria (738.5/261.5)
Two fountains but no other facilities. *Monastery church (double-towered building outside village), parish church (note the painted wooden relief sculptures on church and sacristy doors: one of Saints Peter and Paul, the others of the seven sinners in the fiery furnace). Painted reredos inside with representation of San Roque.*

2.5km Triufé (741/259)
Fountain. *Village still has house that was once the pilgrim hospital.*

4km Puebla de Sanabria 960m (745/255)
All facilities, RENFE 1km above the town at top of hill (Madrid, Zamora, Ourense, Santiago), buses (from petrol station on main road 1km outside town) to Madrid, Zamora, Pontevedra and various other parts of Galicia.

Room (and hot showers) reported available to pilgrims in *ayuntamiento* (ask there or in Tourist office?) Several hotels, HS la Trucha, Ctra Vieja de Vigo (in newer part of town, tel: 980.62.00.60 and 980.62.01.50), HR Peamar, Plaza de Arrabal (tel: 980.62.01.36 and 980.62.01.07), three more hotels on main square but NO *fondas* , CH or R&F. Tourist Office at side of *ayuntamiento*.

Hilltop town founded in AD 569 and which formerly had a pilgrim hospital. Castle, 12th c. church of Santa María del Azoque with Romanesque portal and Gothic vault with sculptured scallop keystones above the altar (open July to September, 10am to 1pm and 5 to 8pm except Mondays).

9.5km Terroso (754.5/245.5) No facilities. *Romanesque church of Santiago 500m before village (note scallop shells on doors).*

2.5km Requejo de Sanabria 757/243)
Shops, Hotel Maité (980.62.25.09), Hostal Tui Casa (980.62.24.20, on mai road out of village), Rte Plaza (in centre). PS in *ayuntamiento* (R&F available there? Info welcome).
Church of San Lorenzo. From here onwards you will see many houses with a patín

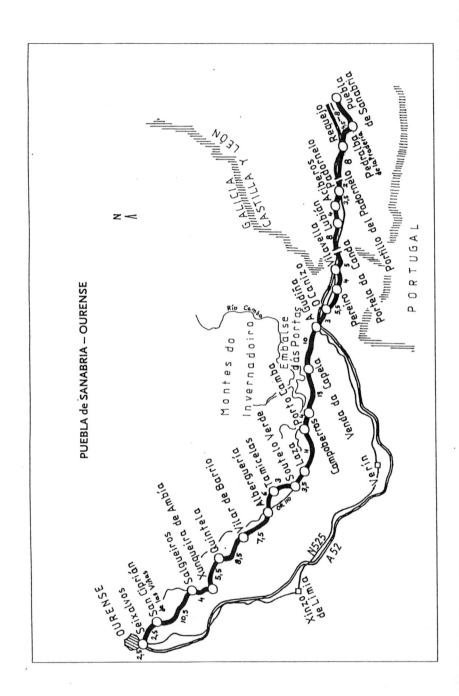

PUEBLA de SANABRIA – OURENSE

(small outside stone staircase leading to balcony and/or first floor, with a landing halfway up but no banisters).

Note: a *cañada* route has now been waymarked from here (leaves by cemetery), leading up the valley (well) below the route on the old main road. Somewhat longer but very quiet and peaceful, though avoid it after heavy rain as it crosses several streams that do not have footbridges.

13km Portillo de Padornelo 1329m (770/230)
Good views on a clear day with no haze (it can be chilly up here, even in summer).

1km Padornelo (771/229)
Two fountains, two bar/shops on main road. Hotel/Rte Padornelo (tel: 980.62.01.06) by petrol station 800m later.

3km Aciberos (774/226)
Another small village with fountain but no other facilities. Twelve inhabitants in winter though a lot of *emigrantes* return in July and August.

4km Lubián (778/222) Bars, shop, municpal *refugio* (8 pl., kitchen), 2 *Casa rurales* (one of them, Casa Irene does meals) but no rte as such.
Here you will find the first of the special pilgrim marker stones sculpted by the artist Carballo, which indicate the route all the way through the province of Ourense.

2km Santuario de la Virgen de la Tuiza (780/220)
This is the church of the Virgen de la Tuiza, with romerías four times a year; the most important one used to be on the last Sunday in September but has now been moved to August 5th, the feast of Nuestra Señora de las Nieves, when the emigrantes (from other parts of Spain, Europe and South America) take part. 18th c. Baroque church replaces a former ermita on another site (stones brought from there) – rarely open. Fountain.

5km Portela da Canda 1262m (785/215)
A pass, forming the border of provinces of Zamora and Ourense and of the autonomous regions of Castilla-León and Galicia.
Fountain, picnic area under trees. Another "Ourense waymark". Can be chilly up here too, even in summer. Good views on a clear day.

1.5km A Canda (786.5/213.5)
Village with no facilities apart from fountain.

3.5km Vilavella (790/210)
Bar, panadería and shop on main road. Hostal Porta Galega (tel: 988.42.55.93) up on N525 at petrol station. Bar "O Carteiro" also has rooms (tel: 988.42.55.99/42.56.48) but no longer does meals.

3.5km O Pereiro (793.5/206.5) HR Cazador (tel: 988.42.55.96) and Hostal Pepe, both up on main road.

5.5km O Cañizo (799/201)
Shop in main square near church, bar on main road outside village. Hostal Nevada at road KM127 (tel: 988.42.10.85).

3km A Gudiña, pop. 2200 (802/198)
Small town with all facilities. *Refugio* – ask in tourist office or *Protección Civil* (on RH side of main road at entry to town) or phone numer posted on refugio door. Hostal/Rte Oscar (tel: 988 42.10.14) and Hotel La Madrileña (tel: 988.42.10.30) on main street in centre, Hostal Relojero (tel: 988.42.01.01) and Hostal/Bar/Rte Suizo lower down (open 24/24).

Town takes its name from the lady (A Gudiña) who used to keep a venda (country inn) here. Halfway point along the Camino meridional between Zamora and Santiago. Baroque church of San Martiño.

Here there are two sets of waymarks as this is where the two routes divide: the northern, more isolated option, 88km to Ourense via Laza, Vilar de Barrio and Xunqueira de Ambía and the southern one (114km to Ourense) that goes through Verín, Xinzo de Limia and Allariz and contains more monuments to visit. Both are waymarked, the northern one in its entirety, as far as Ourense, the southern route as far as the exit from Allariz and both are equally strenuous. You can, however, pass from one to the other quite easily as there are only 13km of minor road (for cyclists, for example) between Verín and Laza and 7km (also on a minor road) between Xunqueira de Ambía and Allariz

A. Northern Route via Laza

To begin with there is quite a lot of asphalt on this route but it is on a small, narrow road that has almost no traffic at all and that climbs high over the area known as the Sierra Seca, barren exposed hills with splendid views all round over the mountains and the reservoirs below you.

Before you reach Campobecerros you pass four of the remaining vendas (venta in Castilian) of a chain of them that formerly existed along this route, simple inns for travellers to rest, eat and sleep and frequently (like A Gudiña) named after the owner or some feature of its physical setting. Today they are just very small hamlets with hardly anyone living there – the terrain is so inhospitable that most of the population has emigrated, either to Ourense, to other parts of Spain or abroad, though many people return for their month-long summer holidays. Even the Venda da Capela, which was a hive of activity in the 1950s when the railway was built, is more or less 'dead' today, its station no longer in regular use and the majority of the RENFE housing deserted. The railway is only a single-track line (with over 100 tunnels between Puebla de Sanabria and Ourense) but it opened up Galicia to the rest of Spain – slowly – as a result. Nowadays there are plans to replace it with a high-speed line from Madrid (requiring completely new track as the present line has far too many curves for the speeds envisaged by an AVE).

3.5km Venda do Espiño de Cerdeira (805.5/194.5)

2.5km Venda da Teresa 1088m (808/192) *Splendid views on clear days, with the Embalse das Portas visible below on R.*

2km Venda da Capela (810/190)

5km Venda do Bolano (815/185)

7km Campobecerros (822/178) Bar/shop in street // to main one. Bar/rte Casa
Nuñez at top of hill on L also has rooms (988.30.54.21), fountai
*Santiago church with modern statue of the saint as pilgrim in niche above front door
and representation of Santiago Matamoros inside building.*

3km Portocambo (825/175)
*At the top of the hill (the pass, 1km) there is a VERY large wooden cross at the side of the
road, some 25ft/7.5m high. This was donated by the monastery at the Santuario de los
Milagros (some distance to the north west of here) and positioned there on the initiative of
Don Eligio Rivas, the parish priest in Bandeira and very active in reviving the camino
through Galicia, in memory of those pilgrims who died whilst making their way to Santiago.*

5km As Eiras (830/170)
Picnic area with fountain and covered seating at end of village on L.

6km Laza, pop. 3000 (836/164)
Bars, shops, bank, rte on main road. Good *refugio* with kitchen (ask in *Protección Civil*, at
side of *Casa do Concello*).
*Small town famous for it carnival. Late 17th c. church of San Xoán. Pilgrims coming
from Portugal via Chaves and Verín (whether Portuguese or from Andalucía, Extremadura
and parts of the province of Salamanca who had made a detour) joined the northern route
here.*

3km Soutelo Verde (839/161) Bar on road at entrance, fountain in centre by very
large concrete cross.

3km Tamicelas (842/158) Fountain.

Note: **Cyclists**, even energetic ones, should continue on the road from
here to Alberguería.

6km Alberguería 900m (848/152) Pilgrim -friendly bar, "Rincón del Peregrino, in
cenre of village.
*Site of former pilgrim hospital, as the village name suggests. Important cattle centre in
18th century with large population. Today it is almost empty but with interesting
vernacular architecture if you look around. Church of Santa María, with statue of Santiago
inside.*

3km Cross on Monte Talariño (851/149)
*Another place with splendid views on a clear day and another large wayside cross that
was erected in memory of those who died on the Camino, as well as the segadores
(reapers) from different parts of Galicia who, until well into the 20th century, walked this
way (and back) each year en route for work in the cornfields of Castille. This cross has a
pile of stones around its base, added to by each pilgrim who passes.*

5km Vilar de Barrio (856/145)

Bars, fountain, shops, bank. Meals avail. in Bar Carmina (at #17, opp. *refugio*) and in Bar Ruta de la Plata (next to supermarket behind church). *Refugio* at end of main square (ask in petrol station).

Town has scallop shell in its coat of arms. Parish church has a chapel given by the Marqués de Boveda, a Knight of Santiago, and whose house (still standing) was also in the town. In Vilar de Barrio you will see the first of the many hórreos (raised granaries for corn, potatoes) that are a characteristic feature of the Galician countryside.

Cyclists may like to make a detour (12km, via the road to Macedo) to the Santuario de los Milagros (services several times a day, every day, during the month of September); you can return to the route via Baños de Molgas *(hostal).*

2km Bóveda (858/142) Bar, two fountains, shop.

6.5 Bobadela (864.5/135.5) Fountain.

1km Padroso (865.5/134.5)

3.5km Quintela (869/131) Fountain.

2km Xunqueira de Ambía (871/129)

Small town with bars, shops, bank, *refugio* next to sports hall (key from Biblioteca, M-F 9.00 to14.00 hrs and 16.00 to 20.00 hrs, or Bar Retiro every day). Casa Rural in town centre (Calle Asdrubal - Ferreiro 4, 988.43.60.80 0r 626.08.95.61). Rte Saboriño on main street near church.

12th c. Colexiata de Santa María la Real with Renaissance stalls, Baroque "Virgen peregrina" in pilgrim outfit on side altar and 16th c. cloisters. Palacio Episcopal, Casa Rectoral, Museo de Arte Sacro.

Note: from here you can make a detour to **Allariz**, 7km away (road to Allariz/Celanova) on southern option and with hostal accommodation and several interesting monuments *(see page 543below).*

2.5km A Pousa (873.5/126.5)

Two bars, shop. *Note two large armorial devices on façade of small church (on R).*

1.5km Salgueiros (875/125) No facilities.

1.5km Veirada (876.5/123.5) No facilities.

4.5km Pereiras (881/119)

Shop, bar/rte. 600m beyond Pereiras there is a bar on L and another one, also on L, immediately after passing under railway line, plus shop 150m later on L.

2km La Castellana (883/117)

2 bars, 3 rtes. Beginning of industrial suburbs at entrance to Ourense. *(Note stork's nest on disused factory chimney L.)*

2km San Ciprián (885/115) Bars, shops.
To visit the recently-restored Capilla Santa Agueda do not cross the railway line but turn L alongside it, go under a railway bridge and then immediately turn hard R up a FP to the top. Seats, good view of Ourense; large porch is good place for a rest. Afterwards go back down the FP and turn R to pick up the *camino* again.

2km Seixalbo/Seixalvos (887/113)
Bars, shops, buses to centre of Ourense.

3km Ourense (890/110)
Turn to page 53 to continue.

B. Southern Route via Verín

10km San Lorenzo

6km Bridge over the Río Mente

4km Vendas da Barreira
Shop, bakery, bars. Two bars/rte by petrol station on main road leaving town (after turn-off to *Camino*); HR Bar/Rte Catro Ventos at KM150.5 has rooms. *18th c. Baroque church.*

3km San Pedro de Trasverea

1km Miros (2km by road)

7km Fumaces No facilities.

3km Rte "La Piscina" Bar/rte at side of road; good views out over valley and Verín below.

8km Verín
Small town with all facilities. Buses to Ourense, Santiago, Benavente, Madrid and other parts of Spain. Several hostales and pensiones. Tourist Office (and Albergue de Peregrinos) in small restored Casa del Escudo (with large coat of arms on front of building) at junction of Avenida de San Lázaro and Avenida de Vences, on other side of Río Tamega on leaving town.

Verín was formerly a spa town and origin of the "Fontenova", "Cabreiroa" and "Sousas" mineral waters. Churches of La Merced (Baroque) and Santa María la Mayor in centre of town, Capilla de San Lázaro opposite tourist office. The Camino Portugués de la Vía de la Plata, *the variant that "turns left" in Zamora to pass via Alcañices and Braganza, joins the main route again here.*

2km Pazos
Shops, bars. Pass a turning to the hilltop Castillo de Monterrei.

Here you can make a detour, 3–4km each way, to the castillo to see the hilltop fortress village which looks out over the entire valley. This was built on the site of the Celtic Castro de Baronceli and three rings of fortifications enclosed a castle whose medieval walls you can still see, a palace, the 13th c. church of Santa María de Gracia and the 15th c. Torre de Homenaxe (a keep). The complex also contained a pilgrim hospital, which is now being restored for use as a refugio, and is nowadays the site of a parador (luxury hotel).

7km Albarellos de Monterrei
HS Bar/Rte San Xurxo at KM171 at entrance has rooms. Shops, bars, rte, bank. *Church of Santiago, with statue of Santiago Peregrino on south wall.*

3km Enfesta/Infesta A long, straggling village with no facilities.

3km Rebordondo No facilities.

3km Peñaverde No facilities.

4km Viladerrei Bar/Rte César, another bar, bank.

1.5km Trasmiras Shops, bars, rte, bank.

4km Zos No facilities.

3km Boade No facilities.

4km Xinzo de Limia
Small town with all facilities. Buses to Ourense, Santiago, Benavente, Madrid. Three hostales/rte: Orly, Buenos Aires, Limia. HS Nazaira, Fonda Vila.
   Parish church of Santa Mariña has free-standing statue of San Roque Peregrino on RH side of chancel archway inside building and capital of a face above giant scallop shell to R of west portals outside.

4.5km Vilariño das Poldras
Purple notice at entrance to village says "Miliarios", indicating a site to R of road.

1km Couso de Limia
Small shop, bar, fountain, sign "Albergue de Peregrinos 1km".

3km Sandías Bar on N525, bank, shop, farmacia. *Church of San Estevo.*

3.5km Piñeira de Arcos Bar/Rte Novariño 800m before village on N525.

2km Coedo

1.5km Torneiros

2km San Salvador *Small chapel dedicated to San Salvador.*

2km Paicordero Another hamlet with no facilities.

2km Allariz

Small historic town with shops, bars, rte, bank. Hostal Alarico on main street and Hostales Limia, O Mirador and Villa de Allariz on N525 at KM216. Tourist Office by road bridge over river at entrance to town.

Romanesque churches of Santiago and San Estevo both have statues of San Roque Peregrino inside, church of San Pedro, sanctuary chapel of San Beito, church of Santa María de Vilanova (church of the Knights of Malta), Convento de Santa Clara with small museum of religious art. Mozárabic church of San Martiño de Pazó 2km from town. Museo Galego do Xoguete (toy museum).

16km Ourense 125m, pop. 96,000 (890/110)

All facilities, RENFE (Madrid, Barcelona, Santiago, La Coruña, Zamora), buses to Santiago, Madrid and other parts of Spain. Plenty of accommodation in all price brackets. *Refugio* (with kitchen) is up on the hill above the cathedral in part of the Convento San Francisco (it shares the building with an art gallery; for opening times and contact see details on door or ask in tourist office, Rúa As Burgas 12, when open). Bike repairs: Pazo de Bicicletas, Avenida de Zamora 2.

The largest town on the route between Zamora and Santiago, situated on the Río Miño. Ourense takes its name from the Roman Aquae Urientes, its hot springs still in evidence today at "As Burgas" near the market and in the termas (spa) alongside the banks of the Miño to the west after crossing the Ponte Vella (old bridge); you can bathe (free) in the hot springs in the open air (bathing suit and cap needed) or pay to go into the Termas a little further along. Ourense was renamed Sedes Auriensis in the 4th century and was the residence of the Suebian kings in the 6th and 7th centuries. Its several places of interest include the Romanesque Cathedral of San Martiño with 13th c. Portico del Paraíso (which includes a seated statue of Santiago), an echo of Maestro Mateo's Pórtico de la Gloria in the cathedral in Santiago, and various Renaissance and Baroque side chapels. It also has the 14th c. church of San Francisco (with interesting cloisters) and the Baroque churches of A Trinidade, Santo Domingo, Santa María la Madre (on the site of the first cathedral) and Santa Eufemia, as well as the Praza Maior, and the Ponte Vella, the Roman/medieval bridge over the Río Miño.

Note: if you wish to sleep in the monastery at Oseira it is ***essential*** to telephone ahead (988.28.20.04).

At a junction after crossing the Ponte Vella the route divides again, joining up 19km later in Casa Novas. Both options are waymarked and both are equally steep.

Route A (via Quintela)

4km Quintela (894/106) Bars, rte, fountain on R by public garden.

4km Castro de Beira (898/102) Bar/rte.

1.5km Liñares (899.5/100.5) No facilities. Main part of village over to L.

1.5km Reguengos (901/99) No facilities here either.

4km Ponte Mandrás 905/95) Fountain, bar on road.

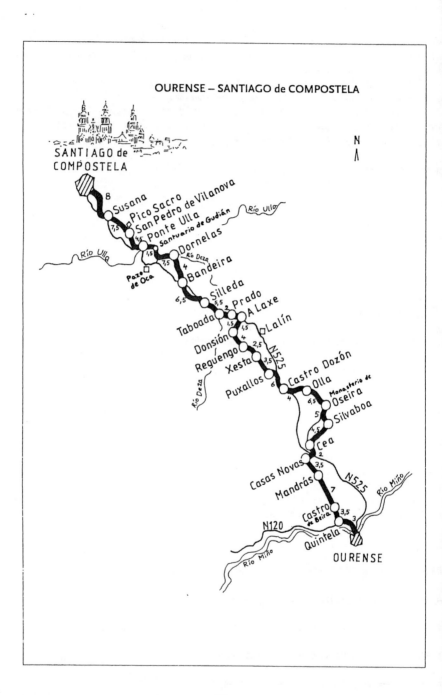

OURENSE – SANTIAGO de COMPOSTELA

SANTIAGO de COMPOSTELA

N

Susana
Pico Sacro
San Pedro de Vilanova
Ponte Ulla
Santuario de Gudián
Río Ulla
Río Ulla
Dornelas
Río Deza
Bandeira
Pazo de Oca
Silleda
Taboada
Prado
A Laxe
Lalín
Donsión
Reguengo
Xesta
N525
Puxallos
Castro Dozón
Olla
Monasterio de Oseira
Silvaboa
Cea
Casas Novas
Mandrás
N525
Río Miño
Castro de Beira
N120
Quintela
OURENSE
Río Miño
Río Miño
Río Deza

8
7,5
0,5
1,5
3,5
4
6,5
5,5
3
1,5
4,5
4
2,5
3,5
6
4
6,5
5
2,5
2
3,5
7
3,5
3

3km Pulledo (908/92)

1km Casas Novas (909/91) Bar O Campo (with sello), shops.

Route B

2.5km Soutelo (892.5/107.5)
2 bars on road.
   Note pazo *on R, with fine coat of arms. Church of San Pedro, with small plaza, has a modern* cruceiro *with sculpture of Santiago Peregrino on its shaft (stick in RH, book in LH, scallops on lapels).*

1km Miña de Chaín (893.5/106.5)
Picnic area, information boards, fountain with very clear water.

9km Tamallancos (902.5/97.5)
Bank, bar, farmacia on main road.

1km Bouzas (903.5/96.5)
Park/bandstand, bar/tabacos, picnic area.
   Old paved stone bridge over Río Barbantíno (note scrolls at each end).

2km Faramontaos (905.5/94.5)
Village that was formerly attached to the monastery at Oseira, with a pilgrim hospital.

1.5km Viduedo (907/93)
Shop, bar. (Turn L to N525 for a bar, with *sello*.)

2km Casas Novas (909/91)
Bar O Campo (with PS), shops.

2km Cea (911/89)
Bars, shops, large *refugio* (42 pl.) with kitchen. *Casa Rural* (Casa Toledo) at Rúa Matadoiro 9 (near refuge, tel: 617.40.04.66). Several bakeries, as Cea is famous for its bread *(Pan de Cea).*
   Parish church in centre and Santuario de Nuestra Señora de la Saleta in field to north of village.
   There are two routes out of Cea, (A) going to Castro Dozón via the Cistercian monastery at Oseira, and (B) going there directly ("por el monte"), both of them about the same length. Read the text that follows before you make up your mind, however, not so much for the routes as such but in terms of where you may want to sleep and the distances you want to cover in each of the three or four days remaining from here to Santiago.

Route A (RH route) via Oseira

(You will also see the yellow and white flashes of another walk – like the French-style waymarks; both sets indicate practically the same itinerary in this section but stick to the yellow ARROWS for security.)

4.5km Silvaboa (916/84) Fountain.

2km Pieles (918/82) Fountain.

3km Oseira (921/79) Bars,shop, campsite by river.
Cistercian monastery built at different periods between 12th and 18th centuries, a National Monument since 1923 and sometimes referred to the as "Escorial of the North" due to its sumptuous reconstruction following a fire in 1552 which left only the church. Most of what is to be seen today (three cloisters, chapter house with curiously twisted columns, plateresque portals) comes from the transition between late Gothic and Renaissance style, often in an interesting mixture. Church contains Baroque altarpiece with carving of Santiago Peregrino by Gambini. Guided visits available.
Pilgrims can stay at the monastery (room, bkft and eve. meal) but only if they arrive before 7pm and **only** *if they ring ahead* **(essential)** *- 988.28.20.04 (the Ourense tourist office will do this for you).*

4.5km Outeiro (925.5/74.5)

2km Gouxa (927.5/72.5)
Bar (marked "tabacos"). First village on the route in the province of Pontevedra.
Note galpón, a long, low covered building with pillars, used to protect those attending the ferias (agricultural fairs) held here and elsewhere in the area; there are very few left now, apart from this one and another in Bouzas (on the RH route out of Ourense).

4km Castro Dozón (931.5/68.5) See below to continue.

Route B (LH route) direct to Castro Dozón

2km Cotelas Shop, bar, fountain.

2km Piñor Shop, bar, farmacia.

1.5km Arenteiro Two bars.
Capela da Nosa Senhora das Neves e Peregrina, a Baroque building restored in 1974 (covered sitting area, good place for a rest).

1km Ponte No facilities.

1.5km Carballeda *Igrexa da Santa María.*

4km Castro Dozón (931.5/68.5)
Two bars, two shops, farmacia. Hostal Castro Dozón at end of village, last building on LH side of N525 on leaving, by municipal swimming pool and campsite. Either R&F (in summer, free) or room, meals, pilgrim-friendly, but reported closed late 2004.
12th c. church of San Pedro.

3km Santo Domingo (934.5/65.5)
Bar/rte. *Church of Santo Domingo (note Oseira coat of arms above main door).*

4km Puxallos (938.5/61.5) No facilities. *Small Ermita de San Roque on R.*

1.5km Pontenoufe (940/60) No facilities.

2km Xestas (942/58) Bar on road.

2.5km Botos de Abaixo (944.5.5/55.5)
Turn L and L again for FF.CC Mouriscade (this is Lalín railway station). Bar/rte and shop. Lalín (all facilities) is 4km away (uphill) on road to R if you want to sleep there (its *hostales* and *fondas* are nearly all in the centre of town).

1km Botos de Arriba (945.5/54.5)

4km Donsión (949.5/50.5) Fountain.
Elaborate cruceiro with figures on base and shaft as well.

1km A Laxe (950.5/49.5) Fountain, new, modern refugio on outskirts of village, directly on *camino.*

2km Prado (952.5/47.5) Bars, one of which, "O Afilador", has rte and rooms (986.79.40.46). Shops.

2km Boralla (954.5/45.5)

1.5km Ponte Taboada (956/44)
10th c. bridge over the Río Deza, in very good condition, with original medieval paved surface dating from AD 912, high above the river for a bridge of this type.

0.5km Taboada (956.5/43.5)
Note *real* scallop shells accompanying waymarks in this area.
Romanesque parish church of Santiago, with a painting of Santiago Matamoros in Baroque altarpiece inside and a modern statue of Santiago Peregrino in a corner of the paved sitting area outside.

3.5km Silleda (960/40)
Small town with all facilities. Hotel/Rte Ramos (Calle San Isidoro, tel: 986.58.12.12), Café-Bar Toxa (on main road, tel: 986.58.01.11),Café-Bar Maril and Hostal González (Calle San Isidoro) all have rooms.

7km Bandeira (967/33)
Small town with all facilities. Refugio 2km before town, slightly off route (no kitchen, but reported comfortable). Hostal/Rte Conder Rey (tel: 986.58.53.53), Hostal/Rte O Portón, Casa Cuiña (a *fonda*) on main road and Hotel Vitoriño (tel: 986.58.53.30) all have rooms.
Bandeira originally had a Hospital de Peregrinos

5km Dornelas (972/28)
Fountain. *Romanesque church with rounded apse (typical of many in this area).*
From here you can make a detour to visit the ***Pazo de Oca***, one of the largest and

most palatial manor houses in Galicia, with its own chapel, lakes and landscaped gardens; continue up to the N525 and turn R onto it at KM315, continue along it for 2km and turn L beside Hostal América *(pilgrim rate reported)* onto a minor road into a thickly wooded valley with the Pazo de Oca at the bottom.

3km Carballeida (975/25)
A lot of very large blue as well as white (wild) hydrangeas in this area.

1km Seixo (976/24)
Bar/shop.

2km Santuario de Gundián (978/22)
Fountain. *Small chapel in a park with a pavilion and sitting/picnic area; good (shady) place for a rest.*

2km Ponte Ulla (980/20)
Bars, shops, rte. Rte Rios (by bridge, tel: 981.51.23.05), Rte Donostiarra Txolo and Bat Tanis all have rooms.

This river forms the boundary between the provinces of Pontevedra and La Coruña (which you are now entering). There are several impressive pazos (Galician manor houses) in this area, which is also reputed for its good-quality aguardiente (a type of brandy).

Notice in gallego after crossing bridge – which you should heed as well as read – says 'Ollo con os cans' – 'Beware of the dogs'.

4.5km Capilla de Santiaguiño (984.5/15.5)
Chapel dedicated to Santiago, built in 1696 and restored in 2000. Fountain with statue of Santiago Peregrino in niche above it. (NB: VERY aggressive small dog in house opposite at time of writing.) Large comfortable refugio reported 100 yards behind the chapel.

*Some 2-3km later you pass a large modern house and reach a T-junction with a minor road. Here the **Pico Sacro** (550m) is some 1.5km away from you, clearly visible ahead, with the 9th-c. Ermita de San Sebastián just below the top; turn R for 1km then turn L to visit and then retrace your steps. This is the place where, according to legend, the bad Reina Lupa (Wolf Queen) lived and who intentionally misled the two disciples seeking a final resting place for the body of St James, sending them to a place she knew to be full of wild bulls that she hoped would kill them all. Instead, however, these animals all calmed down miraculously when the disciples arrived and let them pass unhindered and, as a result, so the story goes, the queen was converted to Christianity.*

7km Susana (991.5/8.5)
Bars, supermarket, farmacia, rte on main road. City buses into Santiago.

4.5km Capilla de Santa Lucia (996/4)
Small church dating from 1829. Seats, trees, good place for a (final) rest.

3km Colexiata de Santa María do Sar (999/1)
12th c. Romanesque collegiate church with inclined internal pillars and very fine cloisters, part of a monastery originally founded in 1136.

1km Santiago de Compostela 264m, pop. 80,000 (1000/0)
All facilities, RENFE, buses to Madrid, Barcelona, Seville and many other parts of Spain. Ask in Pilgrim office about refugios. Plenty of other accommodation and in all price ranges. Two campsites: one on the main road to La Coruña, the other at As Cancelas (on outskirts). There are many places to eat in Santiago but for somewhere cheap, filling and with plenty of choice go to the Café-Rte Casa Manolo, now in the Plaza Cervantes. Tourist Office: 43 Rúa do Vilar (near cathedral).

The most important of the many places of interest in Santiago (all in the old town) is the cathedral, part Romanesque, part Baroque, with its magnificent Portico de la Gloria and façade giving onto the Plaza del Obradoiro. Raised up behind the main altar is the seated statue of St James the apostle to whom it is customary to give the traditional abrazo (hug) when visiting the cathedral for the first time (and which people you encountered along the Camino may have asked you to do on their behalf). The cathedral also houses what is probably the world's biggest censer (incense burner), the famous "Botafumeiro". It is made of silver and weighs nearly 80kg, requiring a team of eight men and a system of pulleys to set it in motion after mass, swinging at ceiling level from one end of the transept to the other. In fine weather you might like to visit the cathedral roof: entrance via Bishop's Palace to L of Obradoiro staircase (8€ for pilgrims).

Guidebooks to the town and its "sights" (in English) are available from the bookshops in the Rúa do Vilar (near the cathedral) or in the new town (such as Follas Novas, Calle Montero Ríos 37). There are also many interesting churches, the Museo de las Peregrinaciones, the Museo do Pobo Galego as well as many large-scale temporary exhibitions. Try to spend two or three days in Santiago as there is much to see and do.

If you have time two pilgrim destinations outside the city are worth visiting. **Padrón** is the place where the boat bringing St James to Galicia in AD 44 is believed to have arrived and also contains the museum of Rosalía de Castro, the 19h c. Galician poet; it can be reached easily by bus (some 20km) from Santiago bus station. **Finisterre**, the end of the known world in former times and the end of the route for many pilgrims in centuries gone by, can also be reached by bus (95km) from Santiago bus station. If you prefer, however, you can continue there on foot, a four-day journey described in the CSJ guide to that route.

NOTES

K.D. Richards is a na
who now lives outsi~~~~
two sons. You can find her at kdrichardsbooks.com

Katie Mettner wears the title of 'the only perso
her leg after falling down the bunny hill'
decorating her prosthetic leg to fit the season. She lives in
Northern Wisconsin with her own happily-ever-after and
wishes for a dog now that her children are grown. Katie
has an addiction to coffee and X and a lessening aversion
to Pinterest—now that she's quit trying to make the things
she pins.

Discover more at millsandboon.co.uk